BEAUTIFUL WANDERER

A SPIRITUAL LIFE IS MUCH CLOSER THAN YOU MAY HAVE IMAGINED.

Sometimes I feel like a wanderer,
meandering through life in various directions.
Running on low, needing a spot to sit and hold someone.
Then I look up to the stark night and realize,
The stars wander and yet their brightness shines on.
I look around and think about my earth,
traveling through space alone on her course.
I think of birds of air and fish in waters,
moving from tree to tree or sea to sea.
All are beautifully wandering to find their way in life,
to find love and purpose and the next place.
I'm not alone in my wanderings,
I'm joined by unnumbered others.
I will wander with you if you will have me,
We can be beautiful-wanderers together...
Exploring the wonders and beauties,
each day never missing a moment...
Loving and being loved,
Lonely no longer as we meander on together...

BEAUTIFUL WANDERER
A SPIRITUAL LIFE IS MUCH CLOSER
THAN YOU MAY HAVE IMAGINED.

Table of Contents

Dedication

I would like to dedicate this book to the Memory of Dr. Wayne Dyer, a man who is still among us in so many ways. I take the baton that you have been carrying along with many others. I dedicate myself to sharing the truths of the spiritual journey that you so profoundly and eloquently shared for so many years. May you continue your work in spirit and may we collaborate still, in reaching the world with the wonderful truth that God is real and alive and all and in all, including each and every one of us!

Entertaining Angels

I am sitting down on a beautiful fall day and starting to write a book that has been inside of me for a long time. I set up my space outside to write. As I prepare to start writing, a white feather blows on my sweater. In most mystical traditions white feathers symbolize the presence of a departed loved one or the presence of an angel, or both.

This week we buried my sister-inlaw, Sylvia, well too young. She had such a vibrant life and was too young from our earthly perspective to leave this world. I am taking this as a sign from God to write and as a clear message that Sylvia is in spirit and maybe will be my muse as I write! I know it is an omen that angels are with me, and I am thankful, for I need their guidance and inspiration to pursue my dream of writing this book.

Acknowledgments

I attribute the writing of this book to so many people who have touched my life. To wonderful loving parents and siblings, to my four wonderful children, to the unnumbered people who were, and are, instruments of God in my life and who's influences have made me the person that I am today. To angels and spiritual messengers innumerable. To one person, who shall remain unnamed, and to whom I owe the intense life-changing promptings to write this book now and to procrastinate no more. You have no way of knowing how much your life has impacted mine. You are the spark that lit the fire.

The title of this book " Beautiful Wanderer" came from the same title of a moving song by Singer / Song Writer / Spiritual Guide and Intuitive Astrologer, Andrea Fisher. Andrea is from Western Australia and she has a world wide impact through her music and coaching that is transformative. Her impact upon my own life has been life changing.

Please click the first link below to listen to the song "Beautiful Wanderer." You will then be able to find more of Andrea's music to enjoy. The seconds link will take you to Andrea Fisher's webpage where you can find out more about her and how she touches lives through her music, coaching and intuitive astrology work.

http://outbackgypsies.com.au/track/732165/beautiful-wanderer?autostart=true

http://outbackgypsies.com.au/work-with-andrea

Introduction

"You see me in everything and that is rare, I love you and you're precious to me. I will use your words, write what you see and feel and your words will give you a beautiful life and I will use your words to beautify others' lives also."

This book is about life, life as a wanderer seeking direction, hope and purpose. Longing for home, but enjoying and embracing the journey. Understanding that life is an adventure to be embraced, not just endured.

I have found that so much of this journey, these wanderings from place to place and from experience to experience, through successes and failures, dreams realized and dashed, is an experience marked with incredible beauty. Every life is beautiful. Every experience adds to this tapestry of divine grace. Even my pain and sorrow and loss has a beauty to it, for it teaches me to let go and to not hold so tightly to anything, to accept my place as a transient being in this world. With eternal origins for sure, and connected to a larger reality than what I'm experiencing in my own journey, yet, holding loosely, everything and everyone.

I want this book to reflect my own life. I want it to look like me. I am a seeker; I am a person who longs to experience all the fullness that I can. I don't seem to be able to accept the status quo. I need something more. I need to see the sky a lot.

I need to feel the mystery of the universe, I long for the touch of God and therefore my journey has been a spiritual one more than anything else. This is what I have to offer the world, a picture of this spiritual adventure that I am calling "A Beautiful Wanderer." This I can give because this has been my life experience.

I offer these words, feeling compelled to do so from deep within and affirmed to do so by many outward signs, an abundance of omens and by the encouragement and challenge of others. I want this writing also to provide some light, direction and hope for you. Maybe some affirmation for who you really are. You see, I believe there are a lot of beautiful wanderers out there, who are just enough detached from this world and connected to another, to need a touch from God. I am writing to you. I am seeking to be used to enhance an understanding of all that has, is and will happen in your life, as an ongoing adventurous journey toward spiritual wholeness and oneness.

I also want to write to you who are tired of a life that seems to have no real meaning, tired of a life that is all about what you have or who you know or how high you have gone. That person who is looking deeper and wondering if there is more to this thing called life. I would like this book to be a light shining into that cracked door. To shine forth a hope and a perspective of life that can be far more rewarding and so much more enjoyable.

You my friend, are a beautiful wanderer, whether you know it or not or connect with the analogy, we all are precious and unique beings with our own beauty to contribute to the larger picture. We are all meandering through life on a path that hasn't always been what we expected, with many twists and turn and surprises along the way and likely many more to come. Maybe today we can embrace this wandering together and find the beauty in it like never before. Thank you for joining me on the journey.

In writing this book, I am following my heart, a divine leading in my life. Some of these meditations will be long and some short, some more spiritual, some more practical, some more of a testimonial and some maybe just observations. None will be exhaustive on the subject but will touch on what my heart feels led to share. I hope you will walk with me patiently as I work through my own wanderings and try to follow the leading of spirit in sharing these words with you.

Think about all the wanderers in nature. The wanderers in the sea and on the land migrate and move from place to place, look at the sky and see if it ever looks the same two moments apart. We may think we are in the same place as yesterday when we look up to the sky but in fact we live on a wandering planet circling through vast space on its course. We see wandering bodies in the universe present their varieties of beauty. No two days are the same, no two moments are the same, and no two experiences are the same. Let your soul expand and enlarge by refusing to be stuck in sameness.

I don't mean to say that you have to change anything in your life on the outside. That may or may not be true. But on the inside, recognize that we are all on a journey from one place in life to another and the road is different for each one of us. The joy is in the adventure of the journey, every moment of it.

I am using the title in this book, A Beautiful Wanderer, because of the incredibly miraculous and beautiful soul that is within each of us and the unimaginable potential for good and greatness and profound beauty that we each possess. Because of the uniquely special journey that each of us is on, not to be compared to another, precious and glorious is your own life and mine as we journey toward our fulfilment. This book is about a journey. It is about me and you and all of us, on this journey together, as beautiful wanderers, experiencing God and sometimes not even knowing that it is God. I pray that this book will enhance and beautify your journey as you see yourself throughout its pages.

ONE

Recognizing the spiritual

Truth and beauty from unseen realms,
Press upon my heart and mind.

A mysterious depth of knowing,
That something magnificent lies behind.

"You think of yourselves as humans searching for a spiritual awakening, when in fact you are spiritual beings attempting to cope with a human awakening. Seeing yourself from the perspective of the spirit within will help you to remember why you came here and what you came here to do"

—The Group, Emilyqoutes.com

All of the great spiritual traditions, mystics of all ages and modern day spiritual teachings agree on this main premise. All substance comes from Spirit. Quantum physics seems to point in this direction also. The idea is that everything physical, including you and me, are in their essence spirit. We say things like, do you feel the spirit of this painting. We spend time observing natural beauty and something inside of us changes. We read an inspirational thought that comes from deep within another human being and we are touched deep within.

We have this unshakable sense of purpose and significance that cannot be denied. We have this longing to connect to something beautiful, truth seeking, creative urges, passion that we must pursue unique to our own soul. These intangible but very powerful, real experiences, come from somewhere.

I align with the ancient mystics. It comes from spirit. Spirit is the eternal energy of life. The creative life giving, purpose driving, beauty and truth behind all that exists. Without spirit there is absolutely nothing, no matter, no universe or universes, no thought, no passion, no creative force, nothing, not even an empty void.

If we are at our very essence spirit, then we have eternal significance and so does every other creature, our life is valuable and purposeful not meaningless and accidental. My passion is my own creative force given to me to make my mark of beauty to add to the beautiful whole.

As long as I can remember, I have had a knowing that there was something unseen behind what is seen that made it what it was. Even as a child, I remember the smell of rain on a spring day and the tulips blooming outside the dining room window and the feeling of joy at a very deep level when the Christmas tree went up and the house was decorated.

I remember my first real awareness of a spiritual reality when I would look up at the beautiful golden angel on the Christmas tree and feel the peace and wonder of worlds unknown.

I would lay there sometimes in almost a meditative state and think about and feel the presence of something unexplainable, a touch of God and an awareness of spiritual realities was being thrust upon me at a very young age. Later in my early youth I began to explore the works of Carlos Castaneda. The idea that the birds or wind or the desert or the sky could be sending spiritual messages to me resonated deeply within as if I knew this other realm instinctively. I later found myself pursuing spiritual vocations as a minister and working in nonprofit organizations with a spiritual component. My entire life up to this moment has been focused on and consumed with all things spiritual.

We can try to ignore this reality or unlearn it or dumb it down but it is there at a deep level in the human experience. In all cultures, all peoples who have lived on this planet, have known and expressed this deepest of human experiences, this knowing of the spiritual. The Mystics and philosophers of all ages have explored and expounded its mysteries to us.

When we think of the inner person, the conscious living being that inhabits the space that we live, we intuitively know, it is more than a machine, that there is a deep place inside much bigger than the physical body that we live in and much more expansive then even the short life span we have experienced. We know it is timeless and we feel its eternalness pressing in on our space time experience.

Just as all matter is really made up of particles held together by vibrational forces of energy that are behind all physics, so spirit is behind all human conscious experience, holding it all together and giving it expression. All that is in the physical realm originates and has its connection to the spiritual.

For my purposes, I am not writing to provide evidence of the spirit to the sceptic. There is plenty of good material out there to research the validity of a spiritual paradigm on life in the universe. My purpose is more aligned with pointing out the experiential markers of such a life and identifying how they work in enabling us to move through life on our journey toward spiritual wholeness. A life connected to and lived in awareness of the spiritual reality, can transform everything, can replace sorrows with joy, hopelessness with purpose and vitality, and fear with faith. Seeing the spiritual realities gives power and meaning to every movement of time and every human interaction and every choice and decision, no matter how mundane or seemingly insignificant.

Try looking at everything in your life, as it is today, from this perspective. See everything as spiritual and your seeing will look a lot different. This book is about the things that you will notice in front of you, as you see your life in this light. As you see your life as a beautiful wanderer, the spiritual realm and all of its aspects will occur to you more and more and become so much a part of your everyday reality.

TWO

Living From the Heart

It has been said that we follow the heart to our own demise,
But the heart will lead to the most beautiful skies.

I would rather follow the hearts deep longing,
Then to heed the conformist's cold calling.

My heart takes me to space deep and wide,
Where my soul can sore and be fully alive.

I will follow my hearts calling today,
And see where it leads along my wandering way.

To live a spiritual life, we must follow the heart. The heart is a term that we use so often to identify this indescribable place within. We all use the term, we say things like, "I feel it in my heart" or "I love you with all my heart" or "you hurt me in my heart" or "that made my heart leap" or "that really came from the heart." We use this term in all of our describing's of this place, this space within us that is undefinable but this space that is clearly our core person. It is not the physical organ that pumps our blood through our veins to keep our body alive, that we are referring to when we say things like this.

We are pointing to a deeper life force, the center of our being. Some call this soul or spirit, for now, we will use the term to mean, the inner most being. That part of me that makes me distinct from you.

The heart inhabits my body as its home and within my heart we find it home to my personality, my emotions, my longings and desires, my fears and struggles, my dreams, my creative powers, my life, my very existence is somehow mysteriously and beautifully there.

I know my heart, my inner sanctum, it is separate from my mind, it is beyond intellect and knowledge, it uses these aspects of me for its purpose but it is being itself. I live and move and have my being, in this inner space called the heart.

A beautiful wanderer is a person who is most distinctively, following the heart. One who is journeying in this inner space and finding truth and beauty, facing fears and darkness, seeding and growing dreams and passions, diving to the depths of being and bringing to the world what we discover there.

It is a journey which takes courage and strength and resolve. It is a journey which will take us through pain and sorrow but also abundance and joy. It is a journey that brings fullness and depth and wonder to life that otherwise we would be missing. I believe it is the very essence and purpose of our being. To explore this deep inner world that is connected to the source of all, to the very foundations and existence of the universe itself.

There is no litmus test. If you are alive, you are a candidate to be a beautiful wanderer. You simply decide to follow your heart and never look back! You pack what little you have, or you set down all the heavy loads that you are carrying and you set out, on the adventure of a lifetime! The explorer in you wants to do it and has been calling you to this kind of life! The part of you that knows your life has deeper meaning and that you are here for a significant reason, this part of you wants to cut all chords of fear and timidity and jump in fully to this exploration.

Through the heart, we can touch the depth of ourselves, God and others. Through the heart, we can find truth and life and love and beauty. Through the heart, we can create something beautiful with our lives. It is the people who live from the heart that touch the world and leave their mark. It is the people that live from the heart that touch the heart of God and bring light to spiritual truth. It is the people who live from the heart that can see the unseen and know what was before unknown. The people who live from the heart are courageous and brave and sincere and genuine, they are often broken and humble as well.

People who live from the heart do things that we never saw coming, they find it within to stay beautiful even when the world is dark, they somehow keep their joy even when sorrow is present, they don't give up or give in and if they do happen to for a moment, they find an inner power lifting them back to their feet.

People who live from the heart have found a higher plane to live from, they leave criticism and judgment of themselves and others behind, for a life of love and grace, knowing that we are all frail and fail and that we all need to return to love when we have our worst moments.

People who live from the heart, will surprise you, they are often beyond stereotyping, don't often fit into a rigid category. They would be easy to pass off as irrelevant if it wasn't for some mysterious drawing power that they have which keeps us intrigued.

I want to be a person like this, who lives from the heart. I want my life to be characterized by all the aspects of what a beautiful wanderer looks like. As we explore this kind of life together, I hope you will be drawn in like I am.

For me to live from the heart, a few things are vitally important. First, I have to say yes to my dreams. To live from the heart means I am saying a big yes! I am turning away from the reasonableness argument that I should not set high expectations for myself so as not to be let down. Forget that! I will pursue the greatness that has been placed within my heart! We all have the seeds of greatness! We all have so much untapped potential, we all have a life calling, this calling may take on many forms but it is ultimately a calling to grow spiritually and become our very optimum selves, fulfilling all of our hearts intentions and imaginings and inspirations, this is our greatest calling and this is the very purpose for our beautiful wanderings.

The dreamer may not be as practical as the rest but she will be the most inspiring! He will be the one we want to emulate and be like! When we see or hear or watch a dreamer, we find ourselves also looking over their shoulder from behind them as they gaze to open horizon with a look of longing and anticipation as they take their steps forward into the unknown armed with one thing, a passion to dream! This is who we all want to be, we can all identify with this figure appearing on the front jacket of this book, and this person is all of us! We all have a beautiful journey ahead and the dream of our soul to fulfill, this is the reason we are here.

Implied in these words is to me the second important step we must take if we are going to live from the heart. We must be true to ourselves. We will look at this more in depth later in the book, for now, we will pay a visit to this idea, by saying, that our truest expression of our love for others is to love ourselves enough to be true to the person, the heart, the dreams, the ideals, the needs of the one person that I am responsible for, and that person is me. It is so easy to forget this and to live our lives for everything and everyone other than ourselves and even think this is commendable.

To live from the heart, however, to fulfill the dreams placed within us in our journey; we must be true to our own heart. We must know ourselves and love ourselves and tend to our deepest longings, this is what it means to live from the heart, to let the person within, be fully expressed and fully lived out.

The expression of what it means to live from the heart will be understood more fully as we explore all the different aspects of what this life looks like. Let's jump in together, no matter where you are in your life today as you read this book. Let's not spend another day waiting to be a beautiful wanderer living from the heart! I'm with you on the journey, let's walk it together!

THREE

Yearnings and Longings

"As the deer pants after the water brook, so my soul longs for you oh God."

Psalm 42:1

Have you ever noticed how people are always filled with longings? Some deep sense of yearning that life is something more. That we are really close to grasping something that is missing but it is just out of reach. Like trying to remember something that we know we know but just can't pull it into the memory. It is right there on the edge of our minds eye. Familiar and beautiful beyond anything we have known. Yet it is undefined, like a translucent image laid over our lives as a blanket.

We have the more definable lines from our senses, what we can see and hear and smell and touch and taste. These are tangible, we use them all the time without effort, but we all are aware of this other sense that something else, so very nearby and with us at all times. This sense creates longing or yearning. We don't even realize that is why under the surface of our lives, we are unsettled, unsatisfied and seeking. We may or may not have struggles in our lives. We may or may not have pain. We could be in a wonderful job and have a generally good life or things may be in disarray.

Yearnings happen to people in all walks and in all stages of life. It doesn't seem to matter how things are in your business or marriage or health. This underlying yearning is an equal opportunity experience.

Sometimes we bury it deeper within because we don't like the unsettledness that it creates. Sometimes we tap into it and allow it to create something beautiful through us.

This yearning is the life blood of the wanderer. It is something that is with us whether we give it attention or not, but it becomes much more dominant if we allow it to have space.

This longing is the yearning of the soul to be given expression, to be allowed to flow, out from within, into the life and personality and experiences of our lives, to lead us to our true selves, to bring out the beauty within and to enable us to create beauty in this world, to connect us to ourselves and to others and to God.

Intuitively we know, we recognize it as an ancient call of God, deep calling to deep, is the way David the psalmist puts it. The originator of the universe, of all that exists, is an alive, glorious and immense being. I am a spark of this being and so I possess a part of God in me.

As a wanderer in a journey of the spirit, I am primarily seeking God. All of my longing can be said to be a longing for God. As a deer pants after the water brook, so my soul longs for God. This is a mysterious and powerful force. It has connection to the beginning of the universe. It can be stated that we have eternity in our hearts and that when we have yearnings we are hearing an ancient and ever present call of the ages to the spirit of all life.

I felt these yearnings as a kid under the Christmas tree looking at the golden angel and as I read the mystical works of Castaneda and as I stood before congregations and shared spiritual truth. I have felt it while looking at a sunset and seeing the orange beams of the sun kiss everything gently before nightfall. I have felt this when I see the emptiness and darkness around me in the world and know at a deep level that life is so much more than this.

This yearning is what calls us to a life as a beautiful wanderer. It is what draws us out and sets us on a course toward the sunrise of spiritual reality. It is what calls me to leave a lesser life and follow.

To all of my fellow wanderers, you are not alone. The truth is, there are an untold number of people just like you and me, waking up to this call from within. There are signs of it everywhere. An awakening is taking place and this book is serving as a part of this awakening. We are becoming aware that the universe has a purpose and that we are all connected in a very real and powerful way.

This awareness and this connection is resulting from wanderers like you and me, feeling this yearning and doing something about it. I cannot ignore it any longer. It is too captivating and it is too strong to just walk by it and not respond. I must act, I must seek, I must pursue, I must follow, I must entrust my life to this deep leading and calling.

The life of a wanderer is the life of a seeker. To have a longing simply means that I am motivated by something very specific and tangible. This spiritual longing of the beautiful wanderer is not haphazard. It is designed with purposes in mind. We are sparks of God yes, but we also have our own soul and we have volition and choice. We will explore later this idea as we look deeply into the nature of love and why we must have a choice to love or love cannot exist.

The beauty and blessings of life are connected to the plan of God for each of us. Not a religious dictate or stifling doctrine, but a life of beauty and love and fullness that we could never imagine. Yet God will not force such a life on us, we must choose a spiritual life. God is there as the source of all that is good and beautiful and loving.

What God does do, however, is plant a longing in us, and plants a desire in us. This mysterious yearning is the spirit of God wooing our spirit. God loves you and me, wants us to know divine love and experience all the beauty of it.This wooing is a loving pursuing of a loving God; this inner longing is love's call from the universe to your soul. I hear it, I feel it, and I sometimes listen to it and often ignore it.

This book explores various ways in which the divine initiates this mysterious wooing. At this moment, just the contemplation that this is occurring is enough for us to consider:

Does this cause your heart to sing, to rejoice, to fear, to turn away? The answer depends on many factors regarding the condition of your heart.

The likelihood is, if you are reading a book like this, something is stirring within you and you are paying attention to it. My prayer is that this book might serve as a magnetic draw to this ancient and beautiful God who is so consumed with the pursuit of your soul that an entire universe has been created for it to occur.

As we journey through these pages, I pray a deeper and deeper awareness of this truth will grip your heart and mind and you will become more and more yielded to the life of a beautiful wanderer. The many souls joining you as well as the multitudes that have gone before make this a well-worn path and one with many markers and provisions along the way.

You will never be alone and never forsaken. What you need at the time will show up at the time. The light for your path will be enough for the next step always and you will never be left in the dark without hope and help.

I am aware that it takes courage to step into the path of seeking a spiritual reality for yourself. Yet anything worth doing takes courage and fortitude. Your courage will be well rewarded.

Let us take these steps together as we move forward on the

journey. Simply saying yes to the drawing of spirit within is the open door needed for many wonderful divine blessings to enter into your life and mine. I am a seeker trying to help other seekers find bread. The bread of life that satisfies the deep longing of souls is ours for the taking.

FOUR

Following Your Inner Compass (Intuition)

"Intuition is seeing with the Soul"
Dean Koontz

Intuition has been called the sixth sense, instinct, inner voice, and many other similar descriptions. It is something we all understand. We have a sense of knowing in our gut, an unconscious knowing. Intuition is active when we fall in love, we know that this person is supposed to be in our life and we are magnetically drawn to him or her. It is active when we get a "vibe" about something that is to be avoided and we can't explain why or we get the same kind of sense that we should be involved with something or go in a certain direction.

What we do with this intuition is a different matter. Whether we follow the promptings from this level of consciousness or not isn't the subject here. The fact that there is this subliminal communication in all human experience is what I'm trying to point out. What or who is talking to us in intuition? Is it the mind? If it were mind alone then we would not have this process that occurs once intuition has presented itself. We may reject the leading of intuition, we may follow it. The consideration occurs in the mind, the decision is an act of will and action that follows. The intuition itself must be from another source. The soul is the logical place to turn. The soul is the real you.

This is the essence of your being, the person inside looking back at you as you stare in the mirror, the part that lives inside the house of the body, giving life to all its members. When the soul leaves, the body dies, because the soul is the life giving principle for the body. The soul is the part of your being connected to the spiritual realm just as your body connects to the physical realm through the five senses, so to, the soul has some senses, that help you connect to the spiritual realm. The soul is the seat of or the foundation of your being. So the soul communicates with the rest of you in many ways, one of which is intuition.

The reason intuition is usually right on is that it has a knowing beyond intellect or ego. It doesn't care about circumstances or others opinions or pressures. It has no fear and limitation. It wants you to tap into your deepest self and know the potential of spirit. So the soul sends out signals to the mind and heart and emotions. When we listen, it's a holy moment.

In my own life I have had many experiences with intuition and have come to rely upon it regularly. There is an ancient story that relates the powerful influence of that still small voice of intuition.

The burning bush moment in the old testament of the bible is a spiritual experience of intuition. Moses was going about his life as a shepherd using his logic and coping skills he had developed. He has a deep sense of spiritual calling from earlier in his life, which he is running from and has gotten good at quieting the voice of spirit.

Yet he knows intuitively that there is something much deeper to his life, much more significant. A long period of trying to forget this knowing for a variety of reasons has created a larger wall to surmount for spirit to communicate with Moses. His pains and struggles and life challenges have gotten the majority of his attention. We too can often become so consumed with life that we forget to really live it. Similar to us, he knew at a deep level that life was something more, but he just didn't give it the attention it needed to produce the spiritual life that was Moses true heritage.

One day, as he walks along a common path on a common day he feels this nudge of intuition. This deep inside feeling or instinct of sense of something out of the ordinary, it calls to him, "Moses, turn off the normal path and go this way." Maybe he stops, recognizes this sweet soul feeling that comes to him from time to time and thinks about doing what he usually does, ignore it and keep pressing forward, head down, no time for turning aside. But today is different, today Moses is listening more closely. Maybe something is happening in his life that has caught his attention.

Moses is listening today and he follows his intuition and turns aside. Once he does he sees the infamous burning bush. In a latter chapter I want to talk to you about the fire of spiritual passion which is represented here. But for now let's just see that intuition has led Moses into a spiritual connection that led to a fresh calling. God spoke to him and called him to be the deliverer of his people from slavery in Egypt. Moses entire life journey was tilted in a totally different direction because of a prompting of intuition and all that happened in the life of Moses after this, was birthed through intuition.

In my own life, the recent passing of my sister-in-law has caused me to listen to this loud and clear prompting to write this book. I can think of many times in my life where something that was happening in life to my circumstances that had me in a more willing position to listen. If you're going through something now that is causing you to dig deeper, to ask questions, to look for guidance, it could be God calling you in spirit, through your intuition.

Steve Jobs called Intuition, "more powerful than the intellect."

Arianna Huffington calls it "the inner voice, which is always there, always reading the situation, always trying to steer us the right way." The U.S. military is even investigating the power of intuition and its ability to help troops make quick judgements during combat, which saves lives.

Intuition is ultimately a communication of the spiritual realm that manifests itself to us in our conscious awareness. We just know, what to do, which way to go, how to respond. This isn't the whole story, intuition alone doesn't make something happen in a certain way and it doesn't take over your will and make you into a certain type of person. It doesn't make decisions for you and it doesn't determine the outcome, but it does prompt you, it does give you the direction that you need when you need it. People who learn to follow their intuition can be said to be incredibly spiritual people then.

They are following an unseen, intangible something that is beyond observation and logic, yet is as real as or more real than anything in the physical realm of their lives. That's a pretty good description of spirit.

In your own life and in mine too, let's agree to be more and more open to this powerful inner voice. Let's recognize how holy it is, it is the voice of God calling you and me into action, motivated by love, and a desire for us to know more and more, the beauty and power of a spiritual life.

So how do we tap into intuition in our lives? What does that look like? What difference does it make when we allow intuition to have a strong place in our lives? For me, tapping into intuition is closely tied to getting to know you, your true self. Not the one we project to others, or the self that we try to be to meet others expectations, but the true you. The most spiritual thing you can do in your life is to get familiar, comfortable and in love with the real you. This is where intuition comes from. Your soul knows what it needs, longs for and is purposed to be. It is a spiritual DNA of sorts imprinted on your inner being and functions as the compass charting your course through life. It is an inner GPS telling you which way to go and which turns to make and when to make them, having destinations in mind that are directed by the universe itself.

It isn't something you do, you don't have to 'figure it all out' it is in you already, placed there by the spirit of all life and it is perfect and infallible. My work is to allow intuition to come through my soul into all of my being.

This is really the work of the beautiful wanderer. It is a process and all of your life is an opportunity for this process to develop and grow into fuller and fuller experience. The life led by intuition will find far more inner strength, peace and confidence. It is not narcissism or arrogance at all, but a confidence in humility that my life is being directed and I am courageously allowing it and following it. It looks like a person with a purpose and an inner knowing that is very profound and appealing, in contrast to a life that is aimless and haphazard and disoriented.

To tap into intuition, we must allow for inner work. Time spent contemplating and meditating and considering the deeper aspects of life. We must allow the spiritual part of us to have some space to grow and develop. We help this to occur as we listen more to our inner voice and less to everyone else's voice. As we learn to trust ourselves and take more control of the directing of our own lives.

Please give space for intuition to grow in you. It will be the most valuable tool in your journey, guiding you along the way toward becoming the highest version of yourself, the very best you can be and the supporting the fullest expression of your potential.

The more time you spend, listening to your inner voice, the more you will recognize it and be able to follow it. I am working hard at hearing and learning from this voice.

I want it to be my primary compass for the directing of my path so that I may experience all that life has for me and not waste time going in circles of my own making or getting off the path by listening the other voices.

Are you hearing the inner voice, are you hearing the loud voices of others that may be contradicting what you feel is right for you? Please for your own sake and the sake of others, follow the inner voice.

FIVE

Finding Faith Through Intention

My inner dream must awake,
It will arise at the eastern gate.

No keeping this beautiful dream within,
A new life of its own it shall begin.

"And whatsoever you ask for, believing, you shall receive".
Jesus

"Our Intention Creates our Reality"
Dr. Wayne Dyer

You have the power to focus your thoughts on what you want your life to be and bring it to pass! Did you read that? Read it again! You have the power to focus your thoughts on what you want your life to be and bring it to pass! This is intention. It is a decision to think in a certain way about certain things that you long for and want to be and deciding to send those thoughts out into the universe in a regular proactive way and rejecting on a regular basis, thoughts that don't fit with your heart's longing and what intuition reveals to you as your souls calling. And then, to see those desires realized, those dreams come into fruition!

Everything that you see with your eyes today was once only a thought! That is an amazing truth. The universe itself was once in the mind of God, an idea of epic proportions. The big bang is nothing more than God's thought becoming a reality through the power of intention! Intellect itself, the idea of thought is something which is beyond the realm of physical. Consciousness is the very essence of God and the very essence of all of life. There is always intelligence before creation and there must be consciousness in order to have intelligence.

So, everything begins in a nonphysical state, intangible, unobservable and yet more real than anything in the physical realm. The computer I am typing on was one in the mind of someone. This book I am writing, it is clear to me, as it comes out onto the page, is already written in the spiritual realm.

Ask any artist, or song writer, or musician, or poet. They all say the same thing one way or another. All feel like something deep within is propelling this onto the page or onto the canvas or into the world.

Think of intention this way. What you focus your thought upon, becomes your reality. Do you see a river that needs crossing and envision a bridge? Someone did, and now we cross rivers with bridges. Where did the idea for a bridge come from? How about just not crossing the river? Why not just stay on this side of the river? Why explore and envision and create and grow and expand?

It is the nature of sprit, it is the essence of life, life grows, life expands, life breathes, life experiences, life requires space and time in order to bring the beauty and wonder of the spiritual realm into reality in the physical.

This is intention! God must love beauty, because everything is beautiful. God must be love because we know intuitively (in spirit) that love is always the best, needed, right thing, even if we don't love.

God must value freedom because we are free will agents who choose our own reality and manifest our own experiences. God must put a premium on justice because we cry out when injustice is allowed to exist. God must be a dreamer because we love to dream. You see all that is, in the seen world, started in something we can't see, touch or put under a microscope.

However, when we do look under a microscope, on the most powerful level known to us, the sub atomic level, or the quantum level, we see a very strange behavior that doesn't seem to match our version of reality. We see atoms, particles of atoms like protons and neutron, inactive until they are observed. The act of observation causes these particles to act in the way that they are acting which is causing all matter to exist.

This is very simplistic description of quantum physics but it reveals a profound truth that is consistent with the power of intention being discussed here. It is the conscious observation of the observer that brings about the action in the matter.

Nothing happens in the physical realm, not even in the most foundational level of the physical universe which makes up all of us and all that exists, without first a consciousness which supersedes all of it, intending it to be. This is spiritual; this is the power we are all given to create the life we are called to live. This is how we are meant to live our lives.

What are you thinking about today? It will become your reality tomorrow. Later, we will explore in more detail, how we manifest what we want in our lives and how important this is to our future, for now, I want us to see that intention as well as intuition, are spiritual principles first and foremost, and coming from a life of following the heart, are the foundational pieces upon which all of life is build.

So with this in mind, here are a few suggestions regarding intentions. Think about what you want your life to become, who you want to be, how you want to impact the world. Define this; your soul knows its own longings. Tap into this, spend time with yourself and get to know what makes you tick. As you develop this personal mission statement for your heart, start to recognize that in your thought life, some thoughts support you and some do not.

Start to train yourself to proactively open your heart to thoughts and input that supports who you want to be, and at the same time reject thoughts that don't support it. You have this power because your thoughts are not the real you. They are a part of you but your soul chooses which thoughts to attach to and which ones to deny.

This happens constantly and when you become more aware of this going on inside, you begin to realize that you have control over which thoughts have influence and which ones you allow to pass.

This can become a life changing awareness. We often think certain thoughts which oppose our inner desires and feel like we have no control over this. To recognize that we actually do have control can be life changing. Similar to channel surfing or turning the radio dial, the soul, the real you, is presented with thoughts moment by moment, from the mind. These thoughts have an unlimited amount of sources.

We have many avenues of intake from the outside world that provides fuel for thought formation in the mind. Things that we read, or hear or see, things others say to us, the list is endless. Not only external but internal sources provide seed for thought formation. Our past experiences, the tape recorder running in the background of our subconscious from early developmental years. The patterns of thought developed from years of input that have created indented patterns that our mind feels drawn to traverse.

We have the power to choose the thoughts presented to us. We can also consciously fill our minds with thoughts that are in line with our intentions and desires.

One is a reaction to what is coming; the other is a proactive filling of the mind with content. In either case, and we will experience the awareness of both, we are seeing the soul at work as the part of us choosing and or activating certain thoughts.

Do you see how powerful this truth is? Can you feel the incredible potential of this in your life? There is no one who determines what thought you see and focus upon and what thought you see and reject, but you, others may have been given that power, but it was and is yours to give and to take back.

This is the key that unlocks the storehouse of God in our lives. When God calls for faith to activate our spiritual desires, this is what is being called for. For you and I to take control of the thoughts that pass through our mind, to place thoughts in our minds which are consistent with the desires and longings which we have and refuse to be dissuaded, refuse to give into those who say you are being unrealistic, refuse the pull of the old self or the draw to self-defeating concepts and ideas.

To believe that I am a child of God with a purpose and that the entire universe is conspiring for my good, and to think on and contemplate and incubate and to incarnate the dreams in me and watch them come to pass. The thoughts literally transform into concepts and then into ways of being and then into attitudes and then into actions and then into a life style. Watch the miracles; see the reality of spiritual guidance and power come to pass in and through your life. This is what awaits the beautiful wanderer when he or she understands the power of intention and the power that we have to create our dreams!

SIX

Living in Inspiration

Like angels from on high,
These fleeting moments come.

When heaven touches earth,
And all things seem as one.

The movements seem to slow down,
Of earth and sky and sea.

As spirit touches spirit,
And my heart and soul feel free.

As I write these words, there is a flow to my mind of thoughts, words, ideas, that I hadn't previously intended. I sense something flowing into me and through me to this blank page.

When I look at the sunset and suddenly feel exhilaration or comfort or peace. I feel a sense that everything is going to be ok. There is a departure of worry and anxiety, an awareness of specialness to this moment.

How do you quantify inspiration? Similar to intuition and intention, it is intangible and invisible but as real as or more real than anything else.

This morning before writing I decided to go to the water front and see the fog burn off. As I approached the water with my camera ready, my heart began to swell with an overwhelming sense of awe. A warmth and comfort and peace combined with a childlike wonder brought me into a trance like moment where the rest of the world and all of its problems and challenges seemed distant and very surmountable as I was caught up in a moment of inspiration.

Most of my writing today will be from the overflow in my heart that has occurred because of this brief thirty minutes spent in beauty and mesmerizing inspiration. It was spiritual and deeply so. As I have alluded to already, all of the great writers and artists and visionaries who have brought so much otherworldly treasures into this world, cannot live, cannot create, cannot fulfill their calling, without inspiration.

A life without inspiration is very empty. Something significant is missing.

Interesting to note, the word used in the New Testament for inspiration, in its original Greek, means... God breathed.

Inspiration can be very easily described as God breathing on human beings, on sun rises and sun sets, on canvases and blank pages, on the otherwise ordinary and mundane moments in life and infusing all of this with life, and fullness and abundance.

How do you explain a cup of coffee by a candle light on a cool fall evening, becoming a work of art? How else do you explain a quiet walk holding the hand of the one you love on any ordinary day becoming a fire in your soul? How else do you explain catching snowflakes like you are eight years old again and getting lost in the wonders of the snow? How else do you quantify the overflow of emotion when you hold the first child or grandchild? How does one explain the magic of fog on water at dawn as the sun rises in the east and the water fowl in the mist frock to and fro?

It's impossible and even illogical to try to describe any of this and unnumbered more moments infused with this something powerful, without concluding that there is some mysterious unseen and yet very clearly known, power, infusing everything with grandeur. It is called Inspiration and it is spiritual and eternal in nature and can be found I'm sure in every corner of this massive and beautiful universe.

The next time you feel inspired, stop and evaluate the experience and see how it affects your entire being. Seek to find and be an inspiration and there will be spiritual fuel in your life that will enable you to be and do and become more then you could ever imagine.

For me, the journey of a beautiful wanderer is one of inspiration. When I think of this life, of beauty and truth, lived from the heart, filled with faith and intentions, I am awe struck. Inspiration is a natural supernatural part of it all.

There are some ways that I infuse inspiration into my life. I proactively work at it so that I can be filled with it as much as possible. To find inspiration I will read poetry or something beautiful, listen to music that stirs my heart, be outside in nature, see works of art, sit by candle light or fire side, play guitar, share intimate conversation with a loved one or friends.

There are so many varied ways to be inspired. Not to mention spiritual practices like prayer and meditation and contemplation. Find things that make you feel good, that raises you up and lifts up your countenance and you will find inspiration. You will know the exalting effect of it more and more as you spend more and more time in inspirational spaces and places internally and externally.

Life is as full as the amount of inspiration you seek to have in it. Since God and spirit are infinite, so are the qualities of the spiritual life. So there is no exhausting of inspiration and being inspired. It can be and is intended to be an all-encompassing part of the human experience and the true flavor of life.

When we are filled with inspiration, we are living from the heart, following our internal compass and living by faith. These all flow together like fish in the same stream.

The result of living in inspiration is a fullness that is beyond the physical, it is a spiritual reality and one that will overflow from your life into the lives of others around you.

You become an inspiration to others simply by living an inspired life; it is not a strong effort on your part to be an inspiration. It is the natural flow of inspiration working its way through you into others.

When life loses its joy or when you experience pain or sadness or loss, please don't forget to allow inspiration to lift you. It always will, it will never fail. You can never go so low that inspiration cannot lift you out of your despair.

One strong wind of inspiration can dispel days or weeks of darkness and it is instantaneous. We do not ignore our pain in such moments, in fact we are propelled by our pain to seek higher ground and to find the overcoming strength and power that comes from the spiritual uplifting grace that inspiration provides.

SEVEN

The Power of Imagination

"Your imagination is your preview of life's coming attractions."

Albert Einstein

Imagine life without imagination for a moment. You can't do it because you just used imagination to try! Imagination is as real but intangible as air. When I was a kid, I lived in a world of imagination. I would stand in the back yard for hour upon hour, pitching a little rubber ball against a block wall. If you happened to be in the vicinity you might wonder why I seemed so mesmerized by this activity. It is because, I was transporting myself to another place through imagination, and my soul was completely engulfed in the experience.

I was really on the mound on 33rd street in Baltimore with 50,000 screaming fans in the Orioles' black and orange. My sweaty cap was all that resembled this but that is where I was for those hours. Zeroing in on the hitters one at a time and making pitches in the perfect location as if my life depended on it.

I loved those hours; they are an important part of my life. I expanded myself there, took myself to worlds outside of my own, and through imagination, experienced things that I dreamed of.

This is why the classic tails like Peter Pan will never die. We are meant to explore the possibilities that seem beyond our grasp, in our imaginations.

I believe that imagination was given to us so that we could tap into the invisible but very real immense world of the spirit. It is a vast world, another dimension, but very real. It makes sense that we would be given the ability therefore, to be transported in our spirit to such a space.

I'm not talking about pretending. I wouldn't say as a child I was pretending either. I was placing myself in a space that I really wanted to be. If the power of intention is true and we do become what we think. Then imagination is the path that intention uses to bring to manifestation, our desires.

When I place myself in the space I long to be in or desire with all my heart. When in my imagination, I experience the feelings, emotions, thoughts, form and place of my dreams. I am making great strides toward bringing my dreams into reality. The reasons for this are deeply spiritual. It is a spiritual principle deep rooted.

When Jesus told his disciples, if you see this mountain being removed, it will be cast into the sea; He was appealing to this power of imagination and describing its effect upon the world of time and space. Imagine the mountain in your life whatever it is, gone.

It could be an obstacle to your growth, a need for provision or protection or it could be your own inability to see past your limiting factors to the dream coming true in your life.

Imagine it gone, imagine no limitations, and imagine yourself in the fulfillment of your heart's desire. Hold that thought, right there, how do you feel? Hold that feeling. This is the power of imagination. If you will hold that thought and that feeling in your heart on a consistent basis, you will find your dreams, mountains will be cast into the sea.

Day dream? yes! Day dream, wake up and place in your mind's eye, your heart's desire, what you long for your life to be and become, who you see yourself as, what you want to accomplish, what kind of difference that you want to make, how you want to impact this world, what you need to overcome, how you perceive yourself to be and what you long to manifest in your experience.

Stop rejecting these thoughts due to fear or because of limiting factors. You may have limits in your current circumstances but remember your current circumstances are the manifestation of what you have been thinking on for the past years of your life. Take responsibly for what is going through the mind and what you choose to focus in upon and give life to.

This is your power. Later we will talk about the power to create and co-create with God, for now I want you to see the power of imagination as a part of this process.

Imagination allows you to escape the current reality and to begin to project the future reality for yourself. Because what you think upon becomes what you are, what you imagine for your life becomes your life.

So day dreaming is not a waste of time for those who can't seem to cope with reality. It is a tool for your spiritual being to participate in the manifestation of your dreams.

Your spirit and body and mind begin to align with your purpose and your dreams will become your new reality. Watch your mind's eye, what is going on in there when your conscious mind seems to disengage from your thinking process. This happens often and living in awareness will help us to recognize this.

Have you ever been reading a book and suddenly you realize that even though the pages are turning in front of you and you're seeing the words that you're actually thinking about the argument you had yesterday or the longing to be with a certain person or a myriad of other possibilities? You grab your imagination and pull it back into the moment and start to read again. Maybe you're driving along and making turns and stopping at red lights and interaction with traffic but it turns out your imagination is somewhere else. You pull it back to concentrate on the road ahead of you. What is happening in such moments? You're imagining. It's almost unconscious at times. We can use this for our advantage. Actually plug in information for your imagination to consider. Don't let it choose its own content. You decide what goes in to your imagination bank.

Make a list of your hearts desires if you have to. You may likely know already what they are and see the list in your mind's eye. Plug in the desire.

Make it specific and set your imagination to work for you. Go for it, sit back while you're driving to work or when going for a walk or when having a cup of coffee in the morning or when lying down for sleep or whenever you find moments to proactively use your imagination.

Think of yourself in the place or as the person or in the circumstances that you long for. Say to yourself, I am a writer, not I'm going to be one day. I am a writer, this is what it feels like to be a writer, you might not know I'm a writer yet, you might not be aware of my book titles and my portfolio, but I'm aware of it and I'm that person because that is who I long to be, that is what I see for myself in my mind's eye, that is who I feel like I'm called to be.

Of course, reality may not match with this yet, but remember that is because current reality was created in the previous moments of imagination. If I see myself as a failure, as unworthy as a limited person who can't accomplish what my heart longs for, I will never become it. If we will regularly imagine ourselves fulfilling our hearts desires, we will start to feel the feeling of it, and feelings are the real driver of the subconscious. Once we feel something, we are going to do it. It has become a part of us and it is imprinted on us now.

Our society has a bit of both mindsets. We promote dreamers as the back bone of our free society. Dream big and you can become anything, but we send mixed messages, we also say don't be to unrealistic, realize your limitations, don't set yourself up for failure and disappointment.

Those are two completely contrary points of view and can and does cause tremendous conflict and can paralyze us and confuse us.

Take control of this process starting today. Do not allow your mind to think in ways that will be contrary to whom you are and who you long to be. You deserve a chance to fulfill your dreams and an opportunity to rise above your own self sabotaging thoughts. You do have this power. No one can take it from you. It doesn't matter where you find yourself at this moment.

You could be behind bars or in a hospital bed or in a rehab center or in the middle of a divorce or business failure or job loss. It doesn't matter, you can start right now to change things, change who you are, change how you view yourself, how you view your future. I am the one who decides, no one else has that power over me unless I give it to them, including my own guilt ridden and self-critical thoughts.

Have you ever wondered if you talked to others the way you sometimes talk to and about yourself, if you would have any friends at all? Are you finding yourself as you think about your inner dialogue, harder on you then you are on anyone else? Harder on yourself than God is on you?

This self-defeating mind set is more than just a mindset. It is a life sentence to staying in your own self-imposed prison of defeat and depression and let down. If this is not changed in you, you will kill your dreams and render your soul, dead in the water.

Please, hear this appeal, your life and future depends on it. The wellbeing of those you love also. The lives of the people you touch every day.

The significance of imagination for your spiritual life is also related to its open spaces and ability to expand. One of the greatest needs of the soul is space. Because the soul is limitless and spiritual, it longs for space even though it is in the body. Imagination gives the soul space which is very much like breathe to the body. It gives life to every cell. When you are limiting imagination you are stifling your soul. That is why it feels all twisted up inside of you and you can't explain why. That twistedness is a soul longing for breathing room. You give it that breathing room through imagination

The soul loves to wander, loves adventure. If you will allow it to wander and take it on some adventures through imagination, the repayment to you will be far more then you gave. All you gave was space and allowance to dream. What is given back is the life you long for and the open hearted largeness of a soul set free.

This space that the soul longs to wander in is very real. It is the spiritual realm. Imagination opens the door to this realm. The wandering is the very essence of spiritual life. We wander because wandering is how we dream and grow and become and know.

Have you ever felt stifled and small and you decide to go for a walk in a park or along a water front or in the mountains. You find yourself feeling larger and the irritants seem smaller.

Your soul is responding to being given space. This is just the nature of who we are. I wonder if that is why the universe is so massive on our scale of measuring things?

I think if we had any sense that there was a point of ending or a point where we could not explore anymore, we would die a spiritual death. God has made the universe large enough that we and any other souls or spirits created throughout this universe, will always be able to explore and wander.

The space within operates on the same principle. It is vast and limitless. When we place self-imposed or societally imposed limits on the soul, we find despair and darkness. Set a people free and they will become great. Set a soul free through imagination and it will repay you many times over.

EIGHT

The Universe - My Playground

"Nature is made to conspire with spirit to emancipate us."

Ralph Waldo Emerson

One thing is for certain and that all of us can attest to. The physical world has a beauty to it and a magnetism to it that is otherworldly. If all that is physical emanates from all that is spiritual, which is a primary principle of spiritual reality, then what we see in nature, reveals something magical and wonderful about the source of all.

God's magnificence is seen in what is manifest from God. When I see the sunrise or feel the breeze gently touch my face or walk along the water or in the woods. When I see the blooming of spring, or summer abundance or the intense and soothing beauty of autumn, the wonders of the snow, all of it points to genius, beauty, truth, love, wonder, mystery, majesty, spirit.

If I were to create my heart's desire with all the giftedness and passion that I have and send it out into the world for all to see, I would rejoice in those who saw it and recognized me. God is alive, real and aware of our response to the wonders sent out into the universe! This thought alone could set the course for life and give you and me a lifetime and beyond of spiritual purpose and awareness.

We can see God in the universe, we can experience God in the universe, we can please God in the universe, we can become like God in the universe.

The soul is infinite and needs space to breath. A stifled soul will leave us miserable no matter what we have or don't have, no matter what our circumstances. If we allow our soul to be stifled we will be empty and unhappy. On the contrary, if we give our soul space to move and to expand, we will find happiness and depth and we will truly live. The universe is a space where we can let the soul expand.

When I stand on the sea shore, bury my feet in the sand and look out over the expanse, several things happen. I am given room to roam within; my soul draws to the open space, to the massiveness of the ocean, to the limitlessness and vastness. This creates spiritual air and my soul breathes in deeply and exhales fully. As I contemplate and meditate and allow myself to be in this moment, my soul can dream and explore and reach and stretch, touching God and remembering its origin and feeling its connection to all of life and to all of the ages of time and space, a part of me remembers that I am stardust and that I am physically and spiritually interconnected with all of the universe and with God ultimately.

As I walk along the shore and am immersed in these powerful moment, my soul begins to worship and praise and I feel joy and exuberance and I am intensely glad to be alive.

I feel the power of the majesty and mystery pressing in on me; I experience revelations and illuminations about life, about myself, about God and about my purpose. I may find direction and answers to some of life's challenges or clarity about a situation that I have been seeking after, or I may have a sense of calling to trust and let go and allow God to have control. I may be prompted to surrender my fight in areas of life or release pain and heart ache. There could be a longing to create, to write, to paint to try to record and communicate what I am feeling, seeing and experiencing, to share my joy, my awareness or my improvements, with others.

I can likely linger in such an experience for a long time, losing track of my normal sense of time. When I do walk away from the shore, I feel at ease or exhilarated or intensely connected or illuminated. I am definitely changed in some way. I am clearly touched by something powerful beyond the elements alone.

What has transpired at the seashore? Nature was used by spirit to communicate, to transform, and to interact with to reveal the deeper reality behind the physical.

In my wanderings, I often find myself in nature. For me, the water is my greatest draw. I always find myself there, I always experience inspiration there, and I always know peace and restored hope when I go to the water. Water is life, the source of all and the foundation of all life. We are made of water and must have it to live.

When I spend time at the water, I am infused with spirit every time. It never fails, I will always experience a touch from the divine and know myself a little better, I will always take something away to give, to create, to share and this allows me to feel purposeful.

I am actually a conduit of divine beauty and truth and life when I'm inspired in nature. It is as real a communication of the power of the spiritual world as electricity is a communication of power of the physical world.

This is why we are so drawn to be a part of nature; this is why it is so important that we care for the earth. It is our little corner of the universe. It is our space to expand and explore. We must protect something so valuable and essential to our very survival. If we view the world and its resources as purely physical, then we are ok with just using its resources for our own consumption. When we do this we damage nature.

Nature if it is spiritual is alive and personal. It has soul, it doesn't want to just be used, and it wants to be respected and honored and understood. We are a part of the natural world. We are not separate from it as we often feel. The advancement of civilization has created this false separateness from nature. As if we can take it or leave it, how foolish of us to think this way. We are a piece of the universe; we really are made of stardust.

Can we separate ourselves from this universe? Can we live one moment without air to breath or sun to give life to all things? Can we survive without food to eat and water to drink?

Can we actually live without sunsets and starry nights? The answer is no, we are a part of nature and it is a part of us. When we abuse nature we are abusing ourselves. When we take advantage of her and disregard her needs, we are taking advantage of ourselves and disregarding our own need. This will only lead to our own loss and hurt.

Sometimes we lose perspective in our lives. We forget who we are. We either get too big for ourselves and begin to feel like the universe revolves around us or we become too small and we feel swallowed up by life. Nature gives us perspective.

Many times in my wanderings I experience moments where I have adjustments like this. The morning of this writing, leaving the house just before sun rise, I started my car and stood there outside of the car looking up. Mercury was bright in the early dawn sky, shining like she was trying to tell me something. I stood and stared, looked off to the west and see the moon in three quarters full getting ready for her rest as sun takes over sky in just a few short moments. Everything above is about to transform from night to day before my eyes, what a miracle, what a moment! As I look at the massiveness, I'm overcome after some meditation that this universe that I'm glaring into is massive beyond my imagination. The numbers are staggering, mind numbing and beyond comprehension. Yet it is real, I am in it, it is all right in front of me. I feel the weight of the magnitude.

If I had any pretense about my own over estimation, it is gone now, yet I'm also overwhelmed with a feeling of significance because I am a part of this interweaving of life and beauty. I am both humbled and exalted at the same time and I walk into my day with the perfect balance of perspective that just so happens to effect everything in my life in a way that, if followed to its logical conclusions, would transform everything in my life, my relationships, my health, mentally and physically, my actions, my priorities, my motivations, my desires. I would treat myself drastically different if I could stay in this state of being, if I could maintain this perspective. I would treat others and the world around me drastically different if I could keep this spirit of balance and illumination.

Nature connects us to God, to ourselves, to others in the way life was designed to be. When we get off track, when our journey gets out of whack, when we need to get back our equilibrium, we need nature to do this. As we go about our life and move from place to place, from season to season, from life lesson to life lesson, remember your point of reference to get back to and stay in touch with God and yourself, is always going to be nature.

Amazingly, even as I write these words and feel the connection to them, I look out the window of my writing space and see birds soaring in open blue sky with bright orange and red and vivid browns along tree lines.

The universe my playground, matching my soul right now, filled with vibrancy and beauty and magical life! I want to experience this connection every moment. I don't want to lose it!

There is also a pace to nature that is very instructive for our lives. A few weeks ago, I went to the water to write. I soon felt led to put down my writing materials and just be in the moment, watching the sky, and the birds and the water and life in front of me. I don't often do this and need to do it much more. I stayed there for five hours which for me is almost a miracle! I got connected to the pace of things and this takes time. It takes time because I am often on my own circumference rotating around my schedule and my pace of things. Yet nature has its own pace, and since I am a part of nature, it would make sense that I find that pace. Since the universe is emanating from spirit then the pace of it must be the pace of spirit. If this is true then it is even more important for me to find its pace and make it my own.

I noticed that there is a rhythm to everything, the way the birds communicate, their flocking to and fro in grouping that seem haphazard but in actuality, have a purpose and reason. The waves from the bay and their hypnotizing rhythmic touching of the shore, the clouds whisking through blue sky creating incredible horizons in all directions constantly changing and each moment a masterpiece. The course of the sun moving through the sky during these hours and an awkward almost dizzying awareness that this is an illusion, that sun is stationary and immovable.

It is my planet, moving, spinning, and tilted rolling through space, glowing in suns light and illuminating its blue hue back into the solar system. I look up into expanse and recognize that the pace is perfect, life giving and perfect, any faster and earth would hurdle into open space and out of the gravitational pull of the sun, any slower and earth would be overpowered by the same gravity and sucked into the suns fiery mass.

Pace is important, it is vital. In modern society we have created a synthetic life and have gotten away from the pace of nature. This has created serious problems for the human condition and has caused us to become separated from our source. We hear the call once in a while. We, in our running to and fro and pushing through life, come across moments of connection, we see the sky and it touches us or we notice a sunset and feel a longing for something mysterious, this happens to all of us. If we listen and follow the leading, we might find ourselves on a healing journey within. Often we just push through, too much to do, to many problems, too much pain, too cynical and too blind by the false reality that we have bought into, to take the journey back to wholeness, to spiritual connection, to God, that is made available to us maybe hundreds or thousands of times along the journey of my life.

My beautiful wandering, takes place in a beautiful space. This universe is my space to live and move and have my being. It is the space that I live, and so do you. I didn't place myself here but I am here.

Let's seize the moment. Like the geese on the sea shore, lets frolic in our giant playground and find ourselves deeper connected to the universe and to God!

NINE

Being Aware of Omens

Signs of heavens presence,
at work for me to know.
That God is always with me,
to help me live and grow.
I will not miss a moment,
of this most precious gift.
To know that spirit guides me,
with signs that lead to bliss.
Today I look for omens,
the universe leads the way.
I will see these wondrous moments,
as the light of brightest day.

The beautiful wanderer needs omens to make it on his/her journey. It is something that he doesn't take for granted or demand, she doesn't ever lose the wonder and awe when omens come her way.

It is yet another wonderful way of the spiritual world at work in our lives, every day, that of signs and omens, these divine indications of spirit at work in our lives.

Literally it can be said, that God is entering into our life experience and intersecting us with an indication of some divine direction, or reminder, or awareness, or faith provoking, experience. When they occur, they cannot be denied and they cause one to stand amazed as we experience an awareness of spiritual reality.

The idea that the originator of all that is, the source of all of the universe, the giver of and sustainer of life in all forms, would interact specifically in my life, by sending a sign of divine presence, with pin point accuracy and orchestration, in ways that are undeniable, is just an incredible and magical part of the spiritual journey. It is invigorating to faith, gives clear direction, and reveals the power of God, the love of God, the wisdom of God, and purposefulness to my life. It brings significance to my own personal existence, takes away fear, and makes me bold in my walk, decisive in my decisions and confident in the outcome. It helps me to project my hearts desires more fully and empowers me to fulfill my dreams, callings and potential. It makes me a better person, more in tune to myself and therefore more in tune with others, I become a better influence on my world and more capable in the hand of God to be used for good in this world. No wonder the universe provides omens for us if we will just look for them.

I have come to rely upon omens in my life. I need to know of Gods directing on my journey. The more we walk by faith the more we will rely upon this divine intervention and the more meaningful it will become.

It is something that is occurring all the time, it is miraculous because it is divine intervention but it is not irregular. Spirit is always working to show us the path and to show us the realness of the spiritual realm.

Some recent events in my life are wonderful testimonies to this spiritual principle. I started this book with an example of omens. I was sitting down on a beautiful fall day and starting to write, I set up my space outside. As I prepared to start writing, a white feather blew on my sweater. The symbol of a white feather in spiritual teachings is most often indicating of the presence of an angel of God in the midst.

Later that day I went into a cafe nearby and continued to write, as I was sitting near the doorway, the door opened as a customer entered, a white feather blew in the door landing in front of me. A week later, I went to the water front nearby and was walking along the water. This day, I had a sense in my spirit to walk and meditate and listen, I went intending to just write but my attention was turned away from writing and I followed the prompting to just be in the moment and pay attention. During a three hour period I encountered two dozen white feathers in ways that were so obviously out of the ordinary.

This is a place I am familiar with and I rarely have seen white feathers there prior to this day or since. One occurrence was as I was walking out to an isolated point, the tip of a little shot of land going out into the bay.

A place I rarely go but felt so impressed to, I walked out to the point and sitting on a large rock, by itself was a perfect white feather right in front of me. This was about the tenth one I had seen and I just stopped there and prayed and accepted the clear directing of spirit. I was in the midst of some very important life decisions and I had followed the leading in front of me a few days prior to go in a certain direction. This day, I was needing some confirmation that I had made the right decision, I felt in my heart I had but others in my life questioned the decision and those who were affected most by my changing circumstances where putting pressure on me. I felt certain standing on this island that God was present with me in a very powerful and real way. I continued to see white feathers the rest of that day. It was so overwhelming.I had no doubt in that moment that God was with me and that I had made the right decision and that my decision was going to lead to my hearts desires being fulfilled!

I have had a few more encounters with white feathers since this day and I have learned more about specific angel interactions in the creative process. I am in the midst of writing this book as this all is taking place. It is an omen that God is with me and behind this entire endeavor.

The same day, after the moment on the island, I felt a leading to go to a used book store in the small town I was in. Something in me told me that the omens where not finished for this day. I had been reading the book The Alchemist by Paulo Coelho.

The main character in this book is seeking his spiritual calling and he is being led to pyramids in Egypt as the place to find this treasure. I have been using this analogy in my personal journey as I project my personal intentions and desires out to the universe. The book and the symbol have become very important for me. I went into the store with anticipation but it didn't know what it was for. I walked around the store for a while and noticed a case with beautiful stones and artifacts. I was drawn immediately to a small crystal shaped like a pyramid. I asked to see it. The store owner took it out and said it was a certain type of crystal from Brazil that was to provide a person with clarity and dreams fulfilled. He went on to talk about more details regarding this crystal and I was blown away. I knew I was to have it. I told him I wanted to buy it. For some reason he gift wrapped it. I felt this gesture was the icing on the cake so to speak. This was a divine gift for me and an omen to find my treasure.

The symbol of pyramid and this type of crystal have opened up into so many different areas and this one omen has led to many others. I expect that more is to come regarding all that this pyramid crystal means for my life.

Omens become an absolute necessity for the spiritual journey. If we are going to live a spiritual life we must have God's omens to help guide the way, to confirm direction and to increase faith. Guidance is a critical part of our life's journey.

If life is purposeful and not haphazard, if the wanderings that I am experiencing are orchestrated for divine purposes, then I must experience guidance. If I'm on my own to figure it out then it's just a matter of chance, but if God is leading the way through the wilderness, then I am being guided and omens are an important part of this.

I must be open, an open heart is one who will receive omens and will recognize them as such. A closed heart will be very hard to reach with these kinds of leading. Omens are subtle and yet obvious. Your attention is drawn toward the sign, often away from something else. You zero in on the sign without even knowing that you're doing it until its right in front of you and then when you retrace your steps, you recognize that you were guided even to the point of being in the right place at the right time to see the omen. This is an important aspect of omens. God does send angels to set up the feathers on the rocks in places that I wouldn't ordinarily go and then leads me toward it with a drawing that I couldn't explain but knew was there, thus setting me up for a moment of worship and acceptance and affirmation in my own little sanctuary on the tip of a small island on the Chesapeake.

I will never forget that moment and others like it. I know in my soul that it was God providing direction and affirming life changing decisions that will affect my entire journey. Without this direction and affirmation I may lack the boldness and determination to move in the direction that I am supposed to be going.

So much good that is accomplished in this world begins with a dream and a leading and omens along the way toward great works of love and light and a world changed. Your life mission and purpose depends on this kind of leading, you seeing it and following it and omens becoming a miraculous and vital part to your beautiful wandering.

Do you see why I call it beautiful? It is a miraculous orchestration by an infinitely wise God, with resources and powers beyond our wildest dreams. God is the dreamer of dreamers, has a dream for you, places it in your soul, causes you to desire it, and then sets about guiding you on the path to find it and fulfil it. Wow, what a miraculous life is this journey. It is the greatest of shames to miss out on the real true purpose behind existence, to know God and all of the wonders of this knowing and to allow God to make your life a powerful and beautiful light to others in this world.

So today, be open to omens. There might be some right here in this book. Somehow, in some way, the universe is going to show up and guide you in ways that you will know for certain, is God coming to you and leading you. As you are living from the heart and seeking the spiritual, as you follow your inner compass and focus your intention on your heart's desire, as you allow inspiration and imagination to be your guides, you will find omens along the way and they will become precious markers on your beautiful journey.

TEN

Synchronicity Speaking

"Synchronicity is choreographed by a great, pervasive intelligence that lies at the heart of nature, and is manifest in each of us through intuitive knowledge."

Synchronicity is another experience that we have in our lives that is tied to a spiritual reality beyond space and time. We all have experiences of synchronicity at times. We could define synchronicity as an apparently meaningful coincidence in time of two or more similar or identical events that are causally unrelated. Those moments in life when things happen that have too many coincidences to be a coincidence.

We cannot produce or predict such moments and we cannot discern that they are occurring until well into an experience of synchronicity. After several seeming coincidences occurring simultaneously we become aware that something interrelated is happening. When we have such experience it is something that we should all respond to carefully. The spirit world is intervening in our time and space continuum with a message for us. It is something important enough to occur several times in order to get our attention. This is similar to omens but can be more prolonged and involve larger circumstances. There can be several people involved over the course of time.

We could look back over the year for example as we think about our new year's resolution and as we mediate and think about the past year, we see a clear pattern of happenings beyond our control and we might become startled as we perceive an obvious pattern pointing to a certain conclusion or direction for our lives.

I might be prompted to start a new business and move to a certain area and as I consider this move and change, I begin to experience a sudden flooding of circumstances from unrelated source that seems to be saying yes to the change and egging me on to go for it.

I remember a season like this for me when I was considering a move to Vermont for a church. I was happy where I was and my family was settled. Over the course of six months suddenly everywhere we looked we saw the Green Mountain state license plates on cars, magazine articles, people walking down the street passing us with Vermont sweat shirts on. Vermont was suddenly everywhere like there was a major marketing campaign in our lives wherever we went. Once we saw clearly that these synchronicities were not random, we began to check into opportunities and within three months, found ourselves and our lives completely changed, living in northern Vermont and pastoring an idyllic little church in the heart of small town New England.

No matter what challenges we faced during our time there, we had perfect unwavering confidence that this is where we were supposed to be.

It was clearly a divine leading for us to go there. The months of synchronicities gave us faith to make the decision to go and were a part of the door opening and proved to be a tremendous encouragement during our time there. Providing needed confidence and affirmation as we walked through our season of ministry in that area.

Without the synchronicities that occurred, we likely would never have gone to Vermont. It is always wonderful to look back and consider the places where God shows up and know that you were supposed to be there. Experiencing synchronicities is a way that we can have the certainty of the universes guidance in life.

Since we cannot produce such moments all we can really do is be open to them which really means being open to the miraculous. It comes upon us unannounced and unprovoked. We did nothing to bring this moment into our lives. It is kind of like deja vu. Everyone has experienced it but no one can really explain it. You certainly don't know when it is coming and yet when you are experiencing it, you know something unusual and out of the ordinary is happening.

You must be open and ready to follow the leading that synchronicities provide. These are moments where God is very near and very active. Ultimately what we are experiencing in these moments is an interaction between the divine perfect nature and our lives in a more obvious way then in the ordinary occurrence of things.

God is always with us ultimately in divine presence but in synchronicities is active and working. A lot gets done in short, powerful moments that can impact a life for years to come. Your entire life can take on a completely different direction, you can experience incredible spiritual growth and have moments that will be sign posts for your entire life, moments you will never forget, you will look back to again and again and relive in your mind's eye.

A release of divine energy has occurred and grace, truth, love, healing, renewal, reclamation and creative force, are left in its wake. These are wonderful miraculous seasons that we should embrace fully and take in every moment, every lesson, and every opportunity for growth, don't shy away or step back, go forth boldly in seasons where God is near. Pray for an increase of and an awareness of such beautiful life giving moments.

A few important factors that make us more open to synchronicities are living in awareness and anticipation. Later in this book I want to look deeper into living in awareness, which really means to stay in this moment. To be in awareness, we are here in the now, looking for the ways in which the universe might guide us and interact with us. We can more accurately recognize patterns of occurrences and will be more able to discern synchronicities.

I know for me, if I'm keeping my spiritual eyes open, I am much more likely to see the ways in which spirit interacts with my life. It is a beautiful, miraculous interweaving and I see it if I'm looking for it.

Don't discount it, if you see a pattern of occurrence, pay attention to it. Be in the moment and sensitive to what is happening in your life at all times.

Another key to experiencing synchronicities is having anticipation of them occurring. Anticipation is related to intention and imagination. Be in a mindset of childlike wonder, knowing that the mystery is going to unfold before you and the universe is going to show up. Something is happening right now that is connected to a larger picture of synchronicities, you can count on it! The more open you are to it and the more you anticipate it the more synchronicities will unfold in your life. You will be living a spiritual life of miracles and nothing will be impossible for you!

ELEVEN

Passion - A Soul on Fire

"Passion is a feeling that tells you: this is the right thing to do. Nothing can stand in my way. It doesn't matter what anyone else says. This feeling is so good that it cannot be ignored. I'm going to follow my bliss and act upon this glorious sensation of joy!"

Dr. Wayne W. Dyer

That which burns in you but never is consumed and never can be extinguished is your passion. In my own journey, I look back from this vantage point, as I sit quietly along the path, and contemplate; I see that what I have been passionate about from a very young age comes from this true and genuine space within me, my soul. I have mentioned my early spiritual leadings in my writing, but at this point, I feel impressed to go a little deeper as I consider the passion that I have, where it came from, what it means, how does one follow it.

I always sensed the invisible side of things. One day, someone put in my hands a copy of a book by Carlos Castaneda. I read it and felt for the first time, that beautiful synchronicity of spirit, when you know deeply something was intended for you and arrived in your life at exactly the right moment. I remember feeling the intense bubbling pressure within that felt like it was going to burst forth. This was the beginning of my passion.

My absolute longing for and love for and intense desire to share, the truths of the spiritual realm. I remember as I was reading and then reading the books by the author and others like him, that I saw everything differently. I went about my normal youth activities, school, friends, playing guitar, sports, social groups, family interactions, but I was different.

I would receive messages from birds and sunsets and the scent of candles or the sound of the wind. I would feel spirit stirring within me and filling me with this intensity. It took over my being, it is all I could think about, and I became aware of God in those days, aware that life was more then what was seen. I spent a lot time contemplating life and death and eternity and meaning and I knew this would somehow be my life's course.

Passion lights the fire in the soul and keeps it burning. Passion drives the soul through the storms and obstacles, passion invigorates faith and uplifts us when we are down by reminding us of our purpose, passion gives our life parameters and meaning, passion makes us feel alive because it is an infusion of life into our very being from the deep part of us, the soul, connected to the enteral spirit and giving us an infinite unlimited supply of spiritual energy and flow.

We will grow weary in our own strength. When life losses its passion we often feel diminished and less then alive. Souls can die before bodies do and this is the worst of all tragedies. This never needs to happen but often does.

When we disconnect from passion and follow either the lead of others or the darkness of losing hope or the cynicism of unbelief, or many other passion killers, we lose ourselves and often describe our lives in that way. I'm lost, I don't know what I'm doing, I need to find myself etc. are all statements coming from a soul that has either not known or lost touch with her passion.

What is your passion? As you think about you own life. What is it that sets your soul on fire? That makes you feel at a deep level, more alive than anything else? Maybe it is several things, maybe you're not sure. Pay attention to what makes you feel like you. What comes naturally to you and others seems to praise you for? It is often hard for us to see it, especially if we have any issues with self-love.

For now, pay attention to that which makes you happy, that which makes you feel alive, that which seems to always be present. It could be a musical talent, or writing or art or doing some act of service, it could be how you create a beautiful space in your home and everyone feels comfortable there, it could be your family and you find yourself at the center of all of the events. It could be a movement of social concern or something to do with the environment. It could be to create awareness about some cause that is near to your heart. It could be, as mine is, to pursue spiritual truth and be a part of sharing this with the world. There are so many types of passion and it is crucial that we all find what we are passionate about because it really is the fire in the soul that will never go out.

If you are in a searching place, trying to discover your passion, stay attuned to your soul. Keep focused on what makes you happiest, what is it that you feel you are good at? What do you love to do and really can't imagine living without?

There is in addition to things we are passionate about, an overriding passion for life itself, for love, for all that is good. This larger passion encompasses the specific areas of life that you are passionate about. Pursue and develop this larger overriding passion as well as seeking to develop the specific areas of life that you have passion in. The beautiful wanderer is a lover of life. We find love in everything and everything has its own beauty. The pursuing of our passion is both our life's work and also our life's essence.

How do you keep from losing it? Passion needs to be protected. There will be people in your life that will try to destroy your passion. You will face obstacles and challenges that will threaten to diminish your passion. There is no place for timidity when it comes to passion. It is a bright fiery light of your soul and it will attract naysayers and it will attract controversy and it will cause you to go out on a limb and take a stand and take risks and often fail and stumble. There will be much that happens in your life because of following your passion that you would otherwise never be able to endure but because of this fire that will not go out, you find perseverance and you find yourself overcoming. It is a power source within you that propels you forward when you otherwise would give up or cower in fear.

You would never have come this far if it was not for your passion. You may not realize just how far you have come and you may not recognize how much of a difference you have made because of following your passion. You are making a huge difference in the world.

I know you're tempted to give up and give in. Don't, it is too much to give up and you know it. Protect what you have accomplished and don't turn back now, you are closer to the prize, closer to the manifestation, closer to the realization of your dream then you have ever been. There is no giving up or giving in, this is your life calling and you are here to fulfil it and nothing can keep you from it now. You have angels by your side and the universe conspiring for your good and all the world is your stage.

Passion will lead you to your calling! There is no one who can do and be what you can do and who you can become! You will fulfill your calling by following your passion and there will be a difference made in this world because of your life. No one can take that away from you. You are here for a purpose and you have been given certain gifts and passions to fulfill that purpose. It is yours alone, no one can take it from you and no one can do what you do.

See yourself today, as you are, a unique and wonderful gift to the world and go about pursuing your passions with abandon, don't fear, don't hold back, this is your moment, this is your time, your season, to shine!

TWELVE

Beauty is My Bounty

Beauty written in the sky,
Beauty written on the sea.
Beauty written in the faces,
Of all the people that you see.
All the universe is telling,
Of the beauty beyond time.
Every precious living moment,
Tells a story so sublime.
See the beauty all around you,
Feel the beauty deep within.
Journey on beautiful wanderer,
A new life of love begin..

A love of beauty is a love of God, it is the same thing, for God is the creator of all beauty and responsible for infusing it into the entire universe including you and me. There is a magnetic pull of the soul toward beauty. Have you noticed? Beauty brings love to the heart. Beauty brings inspiration to the soul. Beauty brings joy to the emotions. Beauty brings healing into the life. Beauty brings light into darkness. Beauty brings purpose to the journey.

When I see beauty, I feel love. This is the primary reason for the creation of a beautiful universe. It is so the love of God can be shed abroad in our hearts. I may be empty and lonely but I see a sunset and suddenly my emptiness is for the moment, filled with love. When I see the beauty of another person, I feel love for that person and for humanity as a whole.

The wanderer is beautiful. When I think about this book and the spiritual journey that it describes, I can't think of a better word for it, then beautiful. It is really a beautiful journey. There is so much intrinsic value in it. What makes something beautiful is its value. We, our lives have been given value beyond compare. We are created in the likeness of God. We are given a living soul as divine sparks, we are unique and wonderful works of creative genius, worked upon with such care and tenderness.

When you see an artist you are so impressed by the love and devotion he has for his work, as much as you are by the work itself. The life that we are living is a continual work of divine love seasoned with grace. It is a beautiful masterpiece. That means that you are beautiful, that means that I am beautiful. We are valued and esteemed highly by the divine creator of all that exists; I need no other affirmation than this. I need nothing else to give my life dignity and beauty. If I will simply be myself, I will be beautiful. I will bring into the world my own unique and wonderful beauty that no one else can bring. There will never be another you.

There is no one who can replace what you bring to the world and your beauty is all your own. The false beauty that the world portrays is nothing compared to this divine spiritual beauty that runs deep within.

My grandmother was an example of this kind of beautiful soul. She seasoned everything and everyone with beauty. She was a beautiful person; she saw the best in others and loved. She was ahead of her time, sang like an angel, could appreciate the simplest things in life and saw the beauty in them. I have many memories of grandmom lighting up when she would hear a song that she loved or when she would have her family around. I remember her offering me as a child, a level of love and acceptance that I felt was different than anything I had experienced. I always wanted her to be proud and when something good happens in my life even now, I wish she was here so I could share it with her and I know she would see the beauty in it.

I remember late in her life I was able to take her to see the orchestra. She was in ill health at the time but I will never forget the beautiful face that she wore that night. Every time I looked over at her she was lit up with a smile that was filled with beauty. She felt every note; she could absorb the beauty of the sounds coming from the tapestry of music. Somehow her illness seemed to take a back seat that night to the beauty that was to be appreciated and experienced.

She had that ability in her life because she was a beautiful soul. She didn't grow old in bitterness and she never lost her appreciation for beauty.

Of course she had struggles and challenges but she faced them not losing her sense of appreciation and love for life. She battled fears and anxieties and moments of darkness, but she was a beautiful wanderer through and through.

I remember when I was asked by my uncle to speak at her funeral, I couldn't think of anything else to say other than that grandmom was a beautiful soul and that this quality was eternal and lived on. That we as her family had a responsibility to carry on her legacy, that we too should aspire to live such a beautiful life.

Edith Locastro, you're my example of a beautiful wanderer and I hope one day when I see you again, I will be able to tell you about my journey and you will be pleased to know that I tried to live for beauty also.

You see beauty elevates the soul to a higher plane of living. If we will look for and find beauty in life, we will see the world as a beautiful place. If we look for the beauty in others we will see others as beautiful people. If we look for beauty we will find it. It is everywhere and it is abundant because it all comes from a beautiful and divine creator.

When we live for beauty we do not live in hatred and we overcome anger and strife. We find it within us to move past hurt and pain and we live for love and to be the best person we can be. We aspire to make a difference, to give to the world not just to take from it. We long for others to be happy and we make our lives a space where people can find peace and acceptance.

We fiercely protect what we love and we defend the defenseless. We are not pretentious and we will not fall for the flattery that comes from manipulative intentions. We can usually see through that and feel pity for the person with such low esteem of themselves.

Beauty illuminates, everything is brighter because of seeing the beauty in it. The sun shines brighter and the sky is bluer. When I look out of the window right now and see the sun setting into a misty cloud bank on the horizon, through early winter leafless branches, I don't just see another sunset; I see a perfectly framed expression of divine beauty illuminated in this scene before me. The ancient steeple of the church across the street reminds me of the men and women before me who were reaching their hearts to the same sky to seek divine beauty and finding as they worshipped together in this space. Beauty illuminates by lifting the spirit to another realm, by penetrating the depth of my being and bringing healing and life and wholeness.

How do we find the bounty of beauty? I think we start by saying yes to a life as a beautiful wanderer. Of course there is a choice, there is ugliness in the world but all that ugliness really is, to be honest, is an absence of an appreciation of beauty. Beauty is the true nature of things. If that is the case then to find the bounty of beauty we just change the paradigm that we are seeing with. It is a change in me not in what is outside of me that will make me into one who can see beauty.

As babies born into this world, we knew nothing but beauty; we had to unlearn it at some point in our life if we are struggling to find it. Children see beauty naturally, this is why they are so beautiful and we are so drawn to their purity and joy.

Childlikeness is a quality that God longs for in us. We are children of God, all of us, no matter how long we have lived and how adult we are, we are still God's children. Sadly sometimes life takes away our natural ability to see beauty. We experience pain or hurt, we are abandoned by someone who was supposed to love us. Somehow life made us lose this quality somewhere along the way. We begin to fear instead of trust and we begin to decline in our ability to see the world as a beautiful place. Of course it was not our fault. The fact the people have choices and often choose to be selfish rather than love has its consequences upon the consciousness of all of us. It is not too simplistic to say that everything is affected for worse when love is not the choice that we make.

We are hurt by life and lose our ability sometimes to see the beauty in us and around us. In some ways the beautiful wanderer is on a journey to restore what has been lost for herself and for all those that she loves and likely for others that are to follow.

THIRTEEN

Truth To Discover

"You shall know the truth and the truth shall make you free."

Jesus

The beautiful wanderer is on a mission to bring truth to all he discovers. Hidden treasures of wisdom are everywhere. The truth seeker never wearies of the search and discovers truth in some wonderful surprising and intriguing places. It is the adventure of all adventures and the wanderer loves adventure.

Truth is not a dogma or doctrine or an opinion held by the majority. It is not a version of reality. It is reality, truth is what is real, how things really are, it is not subjective it is objective. I am not an idealist for saying this. I don't have an ideology that I must subscribe to; therefore I am free to seek truth wherever I can find it. In fact the very concept of an idealist is someone who holds one version of reality against all others and cannot see the truth of anything other than this. Most religions and political movements are made up of idealists. They often didn't start that way. Most of the time a new religious movement or political movement started because there was a calling for and an uprising for change and for freedom from the confines of something that was restricting and or had outlived its purpose.

Jesus himself was of this spirit starting a spiritual movement that was at odds with the religion of his day because it had come to the place of restricting the seeking of truth instead of promoting it. The response of the religion was to have him killed. Jesus and his teachings live on to this day because they represent a seeking of truth as opposed to just a dogma.

A dogma or one way of seeing truth is not truth seeking, this is group mind control. If I cannot think for myself and discern truth wherever I can discover it then it is not truth, it is idealism. Do not sign off on any one version of truth. Allow yourself the open hearted search for truth in all places. This will drive many people crazy who want to define you and categorize you. This gives some sense of control but truth by nature cannot be categorized or controlled.

You can love the words of Jesus and Buddha at the same time when you find truth in their words. The spiritual soul knows truth when he find it and she will not reject it because it does not fit her dogma because she has no dogma. God is too big to be put in our boxes although we spend a lot of energy and time trying to get God into them. God just won't fit! This attempt at fitting God into our boxes has caused us to use God and religion as a tool of our own selfish power and control and has caused the human race major problems throughout history. Please do not confuse this with God. This is man's vain attempts to control the uncontrollable and to define the divine nature in some terms that suits my culture or belief system.

Followed to its logical conclusion, this has disastrous results because the nature of reality or truth, does not match this paradigm.

Wars and hate and division and power struggles and evil itself rises out of such a climate and this is the polar opposite of the nature of God and spiritual principles.

Spirituality and truth seeking that is legitimate does not place such parameters on the search for truth. He searches anywhere and everywhere for the hidden treasure and when he finds it he rejoices! This is what a beautiful wanderer does. He seeks truth everywhere and when he discovers it, he shares it with the world.

As a beautiful wanderer it is your nature to seek truth. As the universe guides your search you will find yourself discovering truth about yourself. One of the greatest explorations of truth that we can partake of is truth about ourselves. This is one aspect of awareness. For me to be able to discover myself and see things about myself is one of the greatest treasures of the spiritual life. It is so easy for me to miss truth about myself and to live out my life oblivious to who I am and why I do the things that I do. To become aware of me is an illumination that will change everything. My spiritual journey will take me on this path of self-discovery. I will be lead on a guided tour of my own nature. This is a prerequisite to being able to understand God and others and the nature of life in general, If I don't see myself truthfully, I will not see anything else truthfully. Be prepared for this self-realization. Do not be surprised in your search for truth that it often is leading back to you.

This is a beautiful and liberating experience and healing, wholeness and well-being will result. Many volumes have been written about what we discover in this introspective truth seeking. In this book, we will leave that open-ended and just allow ourselves to be aware that a large part of the seeking of truth turns out to be truth learned about our own life and nature and history and experiences and purpose and strengths and weaknesses. The spiritual life and journey is a journey into the heart of God. If we are discovering truth, we are learning about this being that we call God, or source, or spirit, or creator or many other names. It matters not what the divine nature is called as long as you recognize that we are talking about the being from which all that exists emanates, the being which is the cause of all causes and the consciousness preceding all reality.

I think and move and have existence and being because of this source of all. Truth seeking and discovery is obviously going to be associated with discovering truth about this being. The nature of God, the character of God, the ways of God, the purposes of God, the person of God are all a part of this truth discovery experience. We are actually getting to know God not just learning about God, we are experiencing relationship to the divine being as we discover truth. Just as we are getting to know ourselves as we discover truth about ourselves. It is relational and personal not abstract and technical. God can be known, this is a miraculous and almost unfathomable thought but absolutely true. The very nature of the universe is set up to reveal the divine being to us. If truth is the way things really are, the true nature of reality, then nature itself should reveal this to us and not surprisingly it does.

We discover truth about the nature of God through nature itself. The universe is one giant magnifying glass showing to us the nature and essence of its creator. God is beautiful and we know this by looking at the beauty of what is made, God is love and we know this by observing that love is the optimum way for all living beings to exist, the complexity of the universe reveals intelligence, the immensity of the universe reveals omnipotence, and the purposefulness of the universe reveals intention.

I do not want to make an exhaustive list here of all of the characteristics of God revealed in the universe itself, that is for another time and place. What I do want to point out is that this universe reveals its originator to us loud and clear if we are looking for it. So we learn about the nature of God as we seek truth, from nature itself.

We also discover truth about God from revelation. God reveals things about the divine nature that otherwise we would not know. Much of the nature of the source of all things is mysterious to us and looking at nature itself does not tell the whole story. The divine being is shrouded in mystery to us because we simply cannot fathom all of the depth of knowing this being fully. We as finite beings and sparks of divinity will spend the ages getting to know the truth about God. Therefore there must be a progression of revelation.

God reveals what I can handle knowing at any given point in my seeking journey. It may take many lifetimes or ages to come to touch the surface of this magnificent being. We are talking about something that we may be just catching a few whispers in the wind in comparison to the fullness of who God is. Revelation is the process that the divine being chooses as we discover what God allows along our journey.

Ultimately though, all discovery of truth about God has to be accompanied by enlightenment. This is the ultimate level of truth discovery. When I experience enlightenment, truth has not only been discovered and revealed, but personalized and incarnated. My person, my emotions and feelings, my thoughts, my will, all of me, has been changed by the truth. I am now an incarnated bearer of the truth that I have discovered. When we experience enlightenment regarding a truth we are discovering, it is as the term implies, as if a light has turned on in a dark room, we now see.

Our consciousness rises to the level of the truth in enlightenment, not just our intellect or our knowledge but our very level of consciousness rises up because we have been transformed. This is the ultimate purpose of the pursuit of truth and why the divine nature calls us to our wandering and searching.

It is truly a continual life transforming experience to be enlightened by the truth that is being discovered, revealed and incarnated in your very soul!

Don't become disillusioned by the battle for truth taking place in our world. Another term for a spiritual wanderer can be a warrior of the heart. We must fight and be strong when it comes to our freedom to be seekers and we must refuse the pull toward falling into defined categories which the world so desperately wants to place us. It can be a lonely road at times and one which takes us up steep climbs and on ragged cliffs. We must keep our focus on the goal and refuse to be disillusioned by what we see at times around us.

The more the light shines the more the darkness will flee but not without a fight. You are on this journey for your life and for the lives of those you love. You seek to raise the level of consciousness both in you and around you and the primary way to do this is to search for truth and wherever you discover it, to allow it to have its full effect in you and through you.

FOURTEEN

Mistakes are God's Methods

"Making mistakes is better than faking perfection."
Unknown

When we find ourselves in this adventurous journey for truth and beauty and as we try to live by faith and boldly walk in this world as a person of heart, following our inner compass, seeking to be inspired and using imagination and intention to follow our dreams and as we seek to follow the signs on our path and pursue our passions in this vast world of ours with unlimited possibilities, we are going to, at times, make mistakes, make wrong decisions, miss opportunities and fail.

I can attest to this personally from my own experience. I have in fact become fairly accustomed to it. Not that I'm looking for it or not trying to avoid it. But that it seems to be a regular part of my life experience and no matter how diligent I am or how I attempt to avoid it, I make mistakes. I go down the wrong road at times, I say the wrong thing, and forget to say what I should say, I doubt when I need to believe and I get selfish when I should love and I have self-pity when I should be grateful and I act when I should wait and I wait when I should act and I leave before I should or I stay longer then I should have. I can't get past the past sometimes and I get stuck worrying about the future, sometimes. I am too impulsive at times and at other times I miss the important door in the moment right in front of me.

If it was totally up to me to find my way through this journey, I would be in serious trouble. I have needed mercy and grace many times, to get me back on track; I have needed fresh starts, gotten them, and blown it again. I have experienced a fresh and clean slate and dirtied it up not long after.

One very real aspect of spiritual growth is failing forward. Learning from my failings, gaining wisdom from the holes I have stepped in, having insight because I recognize the forest and don't want to spend more time there then necessary. I want to get to and stay at the palace. I want to be in the light and keep the channel clean and the water flowing. I do not want to get angry and stay that way, I do not want to let people down and cause them to question my integrity. I do not want to be someone else's reason for giving up or not trying. Yet, my journey often takes me to places where I shouldn't be going and yet I do go. I have made many costly mistakes in my life, ironically, all the while, with a very strong desire to please and to do what is right.

So how could this be? Why would someone who wants to walk in the light and wants to spend every waking moment spreading the light, have so much time spent in dark holes, many of my own making? Spend so much time, rebuilding after mistakes brought down something I built. Some things ended because they needed to and I was often on the other side, making the mistake of trying to keep something in my life that was supposed to be exiting it. How could I get on the wrong side so many times?

One of the reasons is simply this. I didn't know what I didn't know before I learned it. Think about it. If I am going to learn to walk, I am going to fall down. If I am going to live by faith, I am going to experience doubt, if I am striving to love; I am going to have times where I act selfishly. I didn't know what I didn't know before I learned it. Some things must be experienced before they are known. Tell me all day how falling in love young is not wise but I will still fall in love young, then I will be one of those later, saying, falling in love young isn't wise!

I have lessons laid out for me on the wandering path that is my journey and I will learn them for myself. I cannot make your lessons mine or mine yours. I can learn from you and you from me, but we can't substitute learning from others for our own life lessons.

One amazing fact that I want to interject here is this, when I do look at my life and see my mistakes, I can see in most cases why that lesson was necessary for me and I understand that providence was at work setting up the lesson in my life. I'm so glad for this. I need and long for the indicators of divine providence in my life. It is life to me and I live for it.

Another reason for mistakes is a lack of trust. I'm on a journey to learn to live by faith because, ultimately all of my best aspects of my life, my intention and manifestation and passion and purpose, are all tied to living by faith, or to put it another way, trusting in the loving care of the God of the universe that all things are conspiring for my good.

At times in my life, I am confronted with an opportunity to trust and instead, I fear and run from the trust. When I do this, I get off the path of light and slip into a dark space and I am prone here to make mistakes. Some can be costly because I am letting my guard down and not thinking clearly, I am thinking in doubt and fear and I don't see the truth of the situation I might find myself in. When you find yourself in a season of doubt, if you can avoid making decision, please avoid it at all costs, until your light returns. That is not always possible and hence, mistakes are made.

Mistakes can also be acts of rebellion because of hurt. Sometimes, I make mistakes that can be closer to self-willed, self-inflicted, sabotage. I am hurt by Gods apparent neglect in my life, or I am let down by my circumstances or I am reeling from the mistreatment of someone else or I am self-isolated because of rejection or lack of self-love and I carelessly act in ways that brings more pain and more isolation and more hurt.

It is a downward spiral that is hard to get out of. Many people who get in this cyclone never get out of it. They pull down the curtain on every good or potential for good in their lives. This is a place of misery and a place that is very painful to be in or to watch another person live in such a place. There is a feeling of powerlessness to help them stop the pain they are propagating on themselves.

On the other hand some mistakes are an attempt to live by faith and stepping out, and just running out of faith as the challenge mounts.

Have you ever had a strong desire to do something that you felt called to do, God telling you to do? You have a sense of leading, a strong desire, an inner compulsion. You actually mustered up the courage to do it. Things were maybe crazy in the world around you. Others weren't sure what to do but you seemed to see the unseen presence of God in the situation. You seemed to know what to do and instead of being afraid, you found an inner courage to step out and move into the unknown. You did so, with a knowing that all was going to be ok. Others looked at you as you moved forward into the unknown and wondered how you could have such courage. They were afraid for their lives and here you are stepping out into the risky unknown while storms seemed to be ragging around you. There you are, staying afloat by faith and experiencing an exhilaration of faith and certainty.

Then something happens, you wake up at 3 am and look around and see the massive challenge that you're facing and you hear the questioning voices of others asking you to be more practical and realistic. You hear inner voices asking you, what on earth you are doing, sometimes accusing voices saying things like, who do you think you are being so bold and presumptuous. You begin to take in this faith killing information and suddenly lie there in fear and self-doubt. The confidence and boldness you had is gone and now you can't wait for the sun to rise so you can get back to more practical living.

You follow this mindset that has overshadowed your faith and you take it into your life for as long as the fog lingers.

You make decisions or you step back on your affirmations and suddenly you begin to sink. Now, you, like the others who were questioning you, don't know what to do, what to think. At least you have the companionship of the questioners again, accept that they are ridiculing you for your foolishness and belittling your faith which has now come back to earth.

In this state of strong doubt after bold faith (which isn't an unusual experience) you are sinking in the waters and they are overcoming you. You make hasty poor decisions and mistakes that wouldn't have occurred if you were still in the mind frame of faith.

Thankfully the universe doesn't let us stay in this state of sinking and will reach out to us and lift us back to safety, honoring the faith that went before the sinking episode. Yet we do make mistakes during such times and it is a common experience along the path of the beautiful wanderer. I for one am honored to be on the path with such warriors of faith who would trust enough to stand alone at times and to risk all for the sake of the call of the still small voice saying "come."

So accept mistakes as a part of the journey. There is no perfect wanderer. We all find ourselves picking up the pieces of our mistakes and moving forward to what is around the bend. You cannot look back and live in the past, the moment you do, you are stuck. Let it go, let go of your mistakes and see them as a part of the method of Gods building into us the beautiful qualities of the person that we long to be and are becoming right before our eyes!

FIFTEEN

Manifesting with God

From nothing to everything...
Infinite power, glory, blazing from eternity...
Expanse beyond measure,
Brightness of intensity of worlds unknown...
Infused omnipotence into expressions of itself...
Stardust of ancient creative whirlwind still lingering...
Master creator stroking his intense strokes upon the
canvas of time...
Worlds unknown, spheres unseen, colors undiscovered,
 Treasures hidden in the dark depths... Majestic inde-
scribable...
Moment of force and bursting creative genius, with soul
piercing beauty...
So it all begins... So it all is... From glory, for glory, to
glory...
In awe I stand, seeing dimly but perceiving grandeur...
A part of me feels connected to that moment, like I was
there...
I am a piece of the wandering star dust still startled
and spinning
 With reverberations of amazement of what came to be
by the
Act of divine initiation...

All things are because of the manifestation of the divine, the nature of pure consciousness and absolute life. Gods thought becomes Gods act and the universe begins.

A moment of such wonder and glory that a million life times would never unravel all the mystery and power and wonder of that moment. Science has given it the name "The Big Bang," what else can we call it? How big of a Bang was it? What was behind it, how magnificent a moment? All comes from nothing, all of the complexity and beauty and life, and magnificence of all the ages all encapsulated in that moment of beginnings. Before that moment, as far as we are concerned (particles of this original stardust), there was nothing but God.

So everything that is once was not. Creation is the vehicle that brings things from nothing to something. Creation is the means by which all exists. God manifests the divine nature of source throughout all that is made. The manifestation has its origin then, in the mind of God. Think about that, all beings, all life, all worlds, all consciousness, all beauty, all truth, all in the mind of God before it was.

The manifestation of divinity through the universe is a magnificent act of creation. All things which now are, where at one point, a thought, an idea, an unimaginably remarkable one at that! Yet, here it is, look outside tonight and see the stars, they speak and they tell us, this truth. Look at the birds in the air and the fish in the sea and men and women and children and creatures and insects and plants and mountains and fields and rivers and oceans, life covering this planet from corner to corner, circling the globe.

Earth even has a sound, it is the sound of life, and it is alive. Because of this, we are alive, not separate from it. We are here because God initiated this existence that we call life. One of the most powerful moments in a person's life occurs when we realize this truth and then from this enlightened heart, everything appears as it should be. We see the spiritual reality behind all.

God delights in this enlightenment and God chooses to partner with us in a continual act of manifestation. We partnering with God as co-creators. The delight is similar to that of an artist as he stands back, having finished his work and displaying it for all to see, delights in the responses of those who are sharing in his creative expression. This is not pride or conceit. It is the joy of sharing your creation with those that you created it for. This is why the artist spent the hours contemplating what was once only in his mind's eye. This is why the artist brought forth the work from imagination to reality through manifestation. It is for you and me to see and adore and admire and experience the love that the painter has within him demonstrated on the canvas for all to see. He smiles when you smile and he sighs when you sigh, if something in his work makes you cry, he cries with you. It is personal and powerful to him. In a similar way but only in a subtle way this is how God reacts to our response to creation. The difference being that we are not a third party as the people observing the artists painting are, we are the art work, we are the creative outflow, yet we are alive and conscious, God has made us sparks of himself in a sense that we are like the divine in nature and essence. We are spirit and we are eternal. God adores you and loves you; you're the work of the very hands and heart of the creator of all. So the creator rejoices in and with the creature that is made and also is pleased when we adore the handy work of creation. This occurs every time we experience joy and wellbeing and when we love life and are grateful for our existence we actually bring exuberant joy to God!

As if this were not a magnificent enough reality for the spiritual journey and enough to motivate you and I to be courageous and embrace our life as a gift to be enjoyed, I will take it to a new height. One that I have a very hard time comprehending and distilling through my being and that is this. God wants to continue to create and manifest beauty and wonder into the world, through you! Yes, the creator of all that is, the unfathomable being that is the consciousness behind all consciousness, the cause of all causes, this omnipresent all knowing all encompassing being, wants to, has designed all of the principles of the spiritual realm, has set up everything magnificently to, create, manifest, bring forth beauty and wonderful works through you and through me!

The process of God manifesting through you and me starts in the seemingly simplest of ways. A thought or idea is planted. It is a seed of inspiration. Something that God wants in the world and wants to bring through you, simply starts as a thought, over time it marinates into an idea.

This can apply to anything; you plug in what that looks like for you, what you are thinking about these days. What is it that you find yourself wanting to accomplish in the world? It very well could be, likely is God, planting it as an idea, a thought.

As the idea marinades, over time it becomes a desire or a longing. We really want to bring it to pass. Going back to intention, this is where our faith takes over. We put the intention out into the universe and the thought that God planted has ruminated into a desire that we are projecting back to God. This process can take years, not always but it depends often on many factors. However, over time this longing or desire becomes incarnated in you. You see it with your mind's eye. Imagination has created the story inside of you and you now see it all as it would unfold.

This is when it becomes yours. God has transferred the seed of creative thought into you and developed into a life of its own. This is the creative process in all of physical creation as we know. It is also the creative process for ideas and dreams and our life's work and callings. You now feel it moving inside of you, it is alive and it must come out, there is no stopping it from being manifest at this point.

Just as you have been given a physical body to bring forth the propagation of physical life, you have also been given the skill, the abilities, the frame work for the longing to come to pass through you. Your gifts and skill set are not random at all.

You have been made with the exact disposition and abilities to manifest what God has placed within you. You might not see it, you may underestimate your abilities, and sometimes it is hard for us to see our own selves well enough to recognize our abilities. This is one of the reasons that the search for truth leads inward so that we can learn about ourselves and see ourselves the way God sees us. You do have what it takes, partnered with God, to bring forth and manifest your dream.

As the process unfolds, your incarnated dream and calling will find expression in your gifts and skills and then the providence of God will provide the canvas. The dream cannot remain inside any more than a new child can remain in the womb when the time of birth is at hand. It must come out. Your dream, your calling, your longing, must come out. This is the season for it, the time is at hand. Manifestation is at the door, the birth is taking place. Your beautiful wanderings have brought you to the place where God is co creating through you and bringing something beautiful into the world that wasn't here before. It is yours; it is your work and your creation as a conduit of the divine nature, your participating in creation!

Apply this to any form of creative expression, any invention, business development, building, song, ministry, organization, writing, design or development, anything that was not but now is, went through this process.

You fill in the blank. What is in the world because of you? What is coming through you now into the world because you're here?

What is it that you long to become and to do in this world? Your partner in the business, the writing, the venture, the development, the creation, the masterpiece, is God.

This manifestation process is profound and multifaceted and different in every situation but the principles remain the same. We are living out the dream of God, the dream that God had for us when we were created. The dream has become our own and when we fulfill it, it feels like a gift to us and from us at the same time. We find ourselves if we are in awareness, humbled by the process and any success or accolades that comes to us, we will rightly turn to something beyond ourselves and acknowledge this something else, that brought it to me and through me into the world!

Feel it, make it your own. It is only a matter of time before it is in your hands!

SIXTEEN

Miracles, Oh Miracles

"The whole world is a series of miracles, but we are so used to seeing them that we call them ordinary things."
Hans Christian Anderson

Truly a life of God manifesting through me is a life of miracles. This is the flow that we long to be in on our spiritual journey. I now want to explore how God sets us up for miracles. What to look for in your life that can be an indication that God is working the miraculous. It may surprise you that often, challenges, testing times and seasons of uncertainty can be times where God is setting you up for miracles. These seasons where only God can come through are times when we can see the universe do its greatest work.

One of the most profound experiences that we can have in life is when miracles occur. I'm thinking of those beautiful heavenly times when God comes and moves in ways that are clearly divine in origin. Miracles are unexplainable events in our lives that have no logical or reasonable explanation. They most often supersede the normal laws of nature. When my children were born I called each birth a miracle and they are, but for this conversation, I'm really talking about those seasons or events that go beyond explanation and require a divine intervention in space and time.

It's not a hard thing for an infinite, all powerful God to do the miraculous. It's actually common in the spiritual realm. It is a spiritual principle that miracles are a routine part of the way spirit interacts with our lives so that we are able to see spiritual reality actively at work in time and space.

The idea that God cannot be seen and known is foreign to true spiritual reality. God reveals and God works all the time. There is a divine orchestration and ingenious interweaving of events and peoples, and places and circumstances that allow for the stage to be set time and time again for miracles to occur.

In miracles God demonstrates divine love, and power and healing and restoration and grace and truth and beauty to all creatures. Angels, people, events, nature and the most unexpected and uncommon objects can be agents of miracles.

Trying to pin point how and when and why miracles occur is likely a lesson in futility. Once you experience a miracle you can, at times, see the coinciding details of how it unfolded, but to try to explain it or predict it's unfolding in the way in which it does is beyond our perceptive abilities. We can perceive the possibility of miracles and we can propagate them into our lives through faith and spiritual practices but we cannot foresee them until they are occurring and most of the time they happen in ways that we would least expect or anticipate.

The miracle that occurs in my life today has a long life before it happens. It is in the divine mind well before it is even anticipated in my life. There is wisdom and divine purpose at work. Providence guiding lives to certain purposes and ends. Most of the time in the preview of a miracle occurring, God is at work leading the person or persons in which the miracle is going to occur

I'm going in certain direction, I see light in a certain direction and I follow it. This leading, is often accompanied by a strong desire to become more spiritual and less materialistic. It also is accompanied by anticipation of Gods moving in one's life. This longing is coming from God, prompted by God and we are responding to it at a level of spirit within. Remember when you are experiencing spiritual longings and desires, it is God working and setting things in motion for miracles to occur.

The place you find yourself in physically might change as a part of God's miracles. Often God gets us out of comfort zones in order to do the miraculous. Our nature has a tendency to resist change and therefore growth. When we resist change we are actually resisting God because change is the agent that God uses to help us grow in our spiritual journey and do the miraculous work in our lives.

So if you expect miracles, expect change to, nothing growing or living stays the same. We actually are more spiritually sensitive when things are changing. As creatures of habit, we can get into auto pilot and go through life without even thinking about it especially when we resist change.

Have you ever noticed when you drive the same way to work every day, your mind might be a million miles away from the road, the surroundings, the moment you are in. You're so familiar that you don't even notice, you're on auto pilot. You get to work and you don't even remember the ride. Take a new path to work or go on a day trip to a place you haven't been and you find yourself fully engaged, noticing the surroundings and the street names and the towns and the landscape. Because you're engaged you are enriched and feel connected to the day and the moment and the experience.

I'm not saying you have to be moving or finding a new job or on a journey to some unknown place to experience miracles. I am saying that change is often a part of it and this change can be external or internal or a combination of both. When we sense spiritual leading and drawing in our lives, God, the universe, the source of all, is at work, providence is active and this is a season to pay attention. God is always at work, even when things are not energized spiritually but that is another discussion and not a part of this conversation about miracles. So when we are sensing spiritual drawing in our lives it is from God and for a purpose. These drawings can come in so many different ways so don't limit God's avenue of reaching you.

It can be through a book or a song or a piece of art or a person or nature or a myriad of combinations of many things. When this is occurring and we are drawn out, we might be making decisions that needed to be made for a long time, confronting things that need to be addressed, advocating for our hearts in areas that are long neglected and approaching hearts desires that have been long dormant. However spiritual activity is manifesting in your life, it is going to likely cause a shift.

We may find ourselves in places that make us vulnerable or challenged or we may be ready to or actively involved with taking risks in areas that we were static in. Relationships, business, personal growth, creative expression, life purposes, is often in the mix and this can lead us into corners or up against obstacles that we didn't see coming. We may find ourselves following our heart and feeling more alive than we have in a long time. The pilgrim spirit has returned.

As you trail blaze in your beautiful wanderings, you will take paths to places like this. Places where obstacles and corners seem to have boxed you in and thwarted your going forward. Not sure what to do, we look back; question sometimes the wisdom and decisions that got us here. Where is God, why would God allow this? I thought I was following my heart and I thought it was for my betterment. I may look back and miss the comfort of what was.

Even though I needed to change and even though I needed the steps to growth and even though I feel more alive now than ever before, I still feel intensely the vulnerability of this obstacle laden experience and I long for certainty again.

What I don't recognize at this critical moment, is that God is setting things up for a miracle. It is not by accident that I am cornered or in a situation where I need something that I don't have or can't do. If I could do it, I don't need God and I don't see miracles!! Do you see why we face the impossible? It is so the spiritual reality of the universe can come crashing in on my life as God moves the obstacle out of my way. I look at the impossible and I say it is possible with God and I won't back down and shy away, I stand firm and trust even when fear takes hold and even with a knowledge that I have come too far out to go back and that God must come through or I'm sinking. It is time for God to act, when I can do no more or when I am fully surrendered to and open to God acting.

A time for God to act, for the universe to step in, is a time for a miracle. Now God moves! For God it is normal function of divine interaction with created order. For us it is a miracle because divine intervention occurs. God acts by removing the obstacle that was in your way, or by making a way when there wasn't a way to move forward, by providing an answer to a prayer and a provision for a need. It is a miracle because God is doing it and it is my miracle because God is doing it in me and through me.

No one can experience it like I am. I see it, feel it and know it at a deep level. I have witnessed God at work and I am overwhelmed. I am filled with awe. I feel spiritually connected like never before. I praise God for it, tell others about it and it changes my life in sometimes dramatic ways. My faith is stronger and my sense of spiritual understanding, illuminated. God is more real to me in such moments that I sometimes memorialize it, I take some physical symbol of the place where it occurred to remember it by or I set up a monument there for others to know that something divine happened.

Human history is filled with these symbols and memorials, in every culture and land and people groups, no matter the religion or belief system. God has shown up and we acknowledge it in outward tangible ways.

These moments then become markers in our lives. We refer to them again and again, base life direction and decisions upon them, draw strength and grace and courage and insight and wisdom and help from them for years. The miracle occurred in a moment but the effect of it goes on sometimes beyond our lifetime. It can affect generations, cause dramatic shifts in consciousness and awareness and change history.

Often another aspect of our journey associated with miracles is the overcoming of something that previously had us in its grasp. We become freed from limitations which we couldn't change on our own. The slavery to certain vices or destructive patterns is broken and never to be returned to. Real life change occurs and legacies are affected.

In the next chapter we will take a closer look at healing and wholeness in our spiritual journey. History is filled with stories and accounts of this level of transformation due to miraculous life events. My own history, as I look over my wanderings and experiences have markers where miracles occurred and transformation resulted. I'm writing this book in one such period and I am feeling the entire current and direction of my life shifting into a path that I have been longing to be on. Miracles in recent months have opened up a river that is flowing forcefully in a direction that has rerouted my life! I am experiencing this very transformation as I write these words.

Are you facing uncertainty in your life? Are you seeking a deeper spiritual experience on your journey? These types of circumstances and states of being are likely the precursors for miracles ahead. The elements are ripe for a miracle! It's not by accident that you are reading this book and that these words are entering your heart and mind at this very moment.

God is at work, the universe is conspiring for your good. Don't lose heart, don't give in to fear. I know it is scary at times and I know that there is often a paradox between what you long for on the inside and what you see on the outside. Take heart, find space to wait and trust. God is at work and you are not forsaken, healing and wholeness and miracles are around the corner.

SEVENTEEN

Healing and Wholeness

"Crawl inside this body, find me where I am most ruined, love me there."

Rune Lazuli

Miracles on the spiritual journey lead from something to something. Often they lead from brokenness to wholeness in an area of your life. Often they lead to healing and restoration. In this chapter, I want to take a closer look at healing and wholeness in the life of a beautiful wanderer.

Whenever we use the word healing it always implies something is wrong or was wrong. Something needs fixing; some condition is not as it should be. When I think of healing I think of a return to wholeness. It has been said that we are not physical beings having a spiritual experience but rather spiritual beings having a physical experience. If this is true, then there are some aspects of our experience that could be described as a returning back to a state that was once ours. Most spiritual traditions have some kind of description of human beings being a part of a wonderful and magnificent revelation of the divine nature in created form. This is an incredible thought and one hard to grasp. One aspect that would be very clearly a part of such a purpose, would be to create conditions where all aspects of the nature of God could be revealed in an experience that we call human life. There would have to be a way that we could know and experience beauty for example, because the divine nature is beautiful beyond description. We could look at all aspects of divine nature as it has been revealed to us in human history and we can correlate it to some facet of the human experience. Another example would be our passion and innate giftedness to create. One of the most spiritual and yet tangible ways that we display our persons is through the gifts to us and discovered by us to create something. Clearly this is like the divine nature in an obvious way. Again, we could connect the dots to all aspects of divine nature and see it played out in human experience.

When it comes to healing, this reveals an area of divine intention that we need to take a closer look at. The idea of healing as stated above implies that something is wrong, needs to be fixed or returned to a state of wholeness. If we are created by a divine and perfect being then why would we have this experience of being broken or in need of healing? Wouldn't a perfect God create perfect conditions in order to represent this perfection? In one way absolutely this is true, the problem is with the way we define perfection. Let's look closer.

Divine nature is beautiful and powerful and mysterious and ingenious etc. divine nature is also unconditionally loving and gracious and merciful and tender and longsuffering and patient. These later attributes of divine nature require what would appear to be, a less than perfect environment to be demonstrated. What good is unconditional love, when the object loved meets all the conditions?

What good is mercy when there is no need for it? If there isn't an environment where I can fail then I would never need mercy or forgiveness therefore I would never know this aspect of divine nature. God wishes to fully reveal all of divine attributes to us. Yet again the real issue is our understanding of perfect. Perfection to us means an environment free of problems or obstacles or pain or failure, not to mention evil and hate and greed and want. Later, when we look at love as the overriding principle and purpose of the universe, we will look at evil and hate more closely. Think about it, how can one see unconditional love, unless there was an environment where someone would be less than perfect? How would grace ever be revealed if there was not an environment allowed for failure in the human experience? How can there be an environment where we choose the path of love unless there is an allowance for an alternative path? How can we praise the divine nature for being giving and others for emulating this in self-sacrifice, unless there were an opportunity for greed and selfishness? You see, when God allowed divine nature to be breathed into us as we become living souls, we must have the capacity for not living up to the divine nature in order for it to have a true environment to develop. We are not puppets producing output that had been programed into us. We are not inanimate machines; we are living beings with an eternal spirit given to us, a part of us that is the spark of God. In actuality the environment that we find ourselves in for the human experience actually is perfect in regards to having all aspects needed to experience the divine nature.

When I fail, when I hurt or am hurt, when instead of love, I choose hate, or instead of being selfless, I become selfish. Or when I am the victim of someone else's neglect or mistreatment, I have now been placed into an environment where I can experience the grace of God, or the divine mercy. I have an opportunity to understand love at a level that I never could otherwise. Love is longsuffering; love is gentle and kind, and forgiving and unselfish. When I'm hurt because of the lack of those things in my life due to someone's volitional decision to abdicate them, I need healing. I now need the love of God to be demonstrated in my life in its fullness. Not just a love that approves of my goodness but a much deeper love that accepts me in my worst state. This experience that we see as less than perfect and therefore not of God is actually perfect because it allows for the true nature of love to be revealed in offering me healing and restoration.

So having established this environment for healing is perfectly consistent with spiritual principles. Let's talk about life and the
struggles that we experience along the wandering journey. Most of
us that are here for any length of time have experienced pain. We
have known loss, and struggle and failure. It is a common part of our
journey and one that can cause us to either find spiritual awareness
and grow into healing or become disillusioned with life and with any
concept of God.

I used to think this was too big of a risk and if I were God I would
do it another way. Certainly we could find spiritual awareness without suffering? Yet, as we have said, there is no way to know the true
nature of love and the depth of all that love is, without struggle or
loss or pain. There really is no other way. If there was, then perfect
love would take another course in revealing itself.

So let's talk about our brokenness and how we get to wholeness
through healing. All of us come into this world with a pure heart,
open and ready to explore the universe. As we grow into ourselves
and into this world we come across things that close that heart and
discourage that exploration. It could be a difficult childhood, it
could be health challenges or it could be those moments when you
leave the comfort of your protected world as a child and enter into
the world and find it not always supportive to your dream or kind
to your heart. Relationships cause great pain, someone used you,
cheated on you, let you down, maybe many people, you disappointed
yourself by hurting someone else or acting selfishly, financial challenges or business failure or divorce or persecution or discrimination
or control battles in the work place or in the home. God let you down
and your prayers went unanswered or you got the opposite of what
you were praying for.

So many things can lead to brokenness, and when we experience
it, we give up on our dreams, our exploration ceases, we turn within,

or we turn on others and we turn on ourselves and on God.

Fear can take hold, fear of life, fear of death, fear of being left alone and not having what it takes to live in this world. Some take their lives in brokenness; some give up on living but are too afraid to die so they just exist, some become embittered and eventually a shell of themselves.

Every day you and I pass people who are living in brokenness. The world is full of them; you and I may be or may have been among them. It is all attributed to one thing, this brokenness, living in a state of anything less than love.

Sounds simplistic, sounds elementary to suggest all of our suffering can be attributed to one thing, however, it happens to be true. We are made for a perfect state of love and when we or others are not living in such a state we experience brokenness. However, I am not suggesting it is my fault or your fault, this is not about blame, it is actually, as I've stated above, an opportunity for us to experience the fullness of what love really is.

Others mistreatment of me, my mistreatment of others, my mistreatment of myself, disconnection from others, myself and God, all of this is a part of brokenness and creates the need and opportunity for healing.

The door that closed, in my heart, the dreaming and exploring that I was made to be, that has ceased, are the keys to my recovery from brokenness.

It is a life long journey toward fullness and wholeness and this subject is so vast and multifaceted, I would not presume to have even touched or skimmed the surface with these few words of meditation on the subject. However, I can say that these truths are central to our consideration of brokenness and healing.

Open the heart again; all that we need is available to us within, if we will begin to open our heart again. The process leading to a state of our heart being closed can take many years even decades and the process of even becoming aware of it being closed can take as long. If we are fortunate enough to become aware of it, some never do, and live in a state of closed heart and broken spirit the rest of their lives. This is to me the greatest of all tragedies and a large part of what I feel my calling is, to call as many back from brokenness to wholeness as God would use me to reach. Here is the important thing to remember, you can heal, and you can find that childlike open hearted, wide eyed, person again. He or she still exists under all the heart ache and pain and fear and hurt. You're not recreating someone, your actually recovering who you already are in heart and soul and spirit and body, when you are experiencing healing.

To reopen your heart, there are things that need to occur. God's promptings are a huge part of this process. God is prompting us all the time and carefully tenderly trying to help us reopen our heart.

Maybe through the kind words of a friend or a message from a random stranger, or through something in nature, a sunset or beautiful landscape, or through circumstances which are pushing you toward a change, an intervention of sorts in a variety of ways and which I could never describe because it is completely different for all of us, but an intervention nonetheless as God intervenes in your life to promote your healing.

If today you are in need of this kind of restoration or if you know someone who is in this kind of need. Please do nothing before you surrender it all to God and let all of your pain and heartache out to the universe. God loves you and is here for you and wants deeply to hold you and restore you. I know you may be angry or weak or tired and don't know what to do, its ok. You don't have to do anything, just right where you are, sit there, open your heart, let God in, let all the pain out, let healing begin.

EIGHTEEN

Living in the Now

"How much of your life do you look forward to being some-where else?"

Mathew Flickstein

"Walk as if you are kissing the earth with your feet."

Thich Nhat Hanh

As we journey through these experiences of seeking and finding beauty and truth and experiencing God and miracles or healing and restoring. All the journeys lessons and living takes place in this moment, in the now. We are eternal beings living in time, and God is always eternally present in the moment of now. That is one reason that one name for the divine being is "I Am." God fully eternally present now. That is where we always live, in the moment.

All of life happens in the moment. There is no real past or future in this sense. All the past is are moments which have already occurred. It is not a real place. You cannot go back to it. It is not in some kind of time vault or other realm. The future is also not real in this sense. All the future is are moments which have not yet occurred.

We feel so rushed most of the time. This feeling that we don't have enough time is so prevalent in our lives. We often fill our days with activity to the maximum.

We are affirmed by a neurotic society that rewards and honors those who "burn out before rusting out." We kind of sense that this isn't good for us, that in some way, the faster we go the further we are getting from something really important. But once you're on the ride, it's hard to stop it. There is a certain thrill in the speed and we get addicted to it. Like any addiction we justify it. When people ask how we are doing and we answer with, tired and busy but it's got to be this way! We are proud of ourselves in some way and it's almost a crown of achievement to say that we are too busy to breathe.

Never mind the fact that the very pace of nature is far different from this. That our inner person is sending signals all the time to get off this crazy ride. Our bodies also send signals to us in so many different ways. The earth itself is sending signals that we are just starting to listen to. That is another subject for another time but worth mentioning here. Our damage to the environment is a direct result of this misuse of time.

We also mismanage time when we spend so much of it, living in the past or future. Past failures can control our lives until our last breath. We make mistakes, it is a human experience, and it is part of growing and maturing and becoming our best selves. We have taken a look in previous chapters at how mistakes are a part of our search for truth and we have also seen how miracles can include healing from brokenness. Yet, the moment, that yesterday is gone, it will never be brought back.

In the spiritual principle, thankfully we have been given graces to deal with the past failures and pains we have caused. God offers us forgiveness each moment, for each failure and mistake, for each and every hurtful thing we have done or has been done to us. It's not that they are without consequences. We know this; we have experienced the pain of our mistakes and hurtful actions. We have witnessed the pain and heartaches others have experienced due to our actions. But, we can be and are being forgiven. We must forgive ourselves and seek forgiveness from others if it is possible. However you need to apply this, you must experience forgiveness so that you do not live any longer in the past.

Often it is the other way around. It is others hurting you or mistreating you and that has caused you pain and let down. You may feel and rightly so, that your life is less then it could have been or would have been if you didn't experience this pain. It could be a lifetime of such experience and you are completely paralyzed by it and your todays are absolutely tied to and affected by yesterday. I know there are things that we go through that effect our psyche in such a way that we are forever changed. Our very personality has been impacted by these experiences. Our entire existence is characterized by them. We might lose a huge part of our identity if we let go of even the most painful of experiences. Yet, the reality is the same. As long as we hold onto these pains and hurts, we will always be tied to the past and every moment including this one, will be affected by it.

Once again, forgiveness is offered. To forgive others is as hard as, or harder than, seeking forgiveness. I feel and maybe am justified in holding onto the hurt. I am not giving it up for anything. These are my scars and no one can have them is my mantra. It is true; we are forever changed in some ways by the painful experiences of the past. But, we don't have to be defined by them in the present. We can and must let them go whatever it takes. Seek help; work with caring people in your life. Reach out to God and others, whatever it takes, please know that you can release yourself from the past. You don't have to continue to live there.

Another important aspect of living in the past hurts we have caused or received is that, when we do not release them or release others who are associated with them, we are destined to repeat them. It is such a powerful and obvious truth. If I am tied to the past in my soul, in my psyche, I am going to unconsciously see everything in my present through the prism or the paradigm of the past. This is true because I am still living there even though the experience could be five, ten, twenty or more years ago. I am still living it. The tape keeps playing in my mind, the resentments or regrets keep playing over and over like a skip on a record. This is a horrible trap to be in. The greatest danger is that we don't even realize it. It has become our identity.

We have associated reasonings that tell us we don't deserve better, we're not worthy of love, we failed and that's why things are the way they are, someone else is in control of things, this must be my destiny.

All the while, we have the power at our disposal to break out of these chains to a life of incredible freedom!

We can also be tied to the past by living in past successes and accomplishments. Especially if our current lives do not match what we once were. This happens in so many walks of life. After divorce, we feel less of ourselves and compare our current life to that seemingly fuller experience of being a spouse or parent. We may have experienced success in a career path and now are past our peak and or have experienced a career change due to circumstances outside of our control. In this place, we compare all of our current moments to past moments. The former athlete or business man or corporate exec or any number of other tags of significance, and the luster has gone, maybe physical skills have waned or others have become more relevant leaders or still others have been replaced or had to sell or dissolve their once thriving business.

Living in the past keeps us tied to it. We cannot be present in the present and therefore we feel uncomfortable and unsettled in the here and now. Things don't feel right, my spirit is pulling me into it but I cannot release from the past so there is an inner tension and this tension causes the current moment to be unlived and unexperienced.

When I am living in the past hurt or failure or the past success and accolades, I send out into the universe thoughts and feelings associated with what has happened or with thoughts that my life isn't as good as it once was. Either way, we are sending thoughts which are going to create feelings which are going to create reality for me. I am going to continue the same mistake or failure or propagate the same hurt on my life today, the people in my life now. I am going to create a life of let down or hurt or pain because that is my focus.

The same mistake is made when I focus my thought and awareness of future fears and doubts. I would not be one to say don't plan or dream. I have clearly been advocating for that in this book and the very nature of a journey is to move forward. If we are growing spiritually we are moving forward and not living in the past, however, we do this one moment at a time, living in the now.

To be preoccupied with the future creates anxiety and worry or unnecessary frustration and doubt when we can't see our way clearly. We don't need to have the whole sequence of future events explained to us. We live in faith and put our intention out into the universe for our desires and longings to be realized, we imagine them and are inspired and passionate about them. We seek truth and beauty and crave a life as co-creators with God, but we must realize we do so moving step by step and leaving the unfolding to God.

I cannot control the outcome of things I can only control my focus on what I desire as the outcome. The universe takes care of the how and the when.

I will be guided to my desired manifestation as I walk in the moments in front of me in total focus and awareness. Anxiety and worry, fear and doubt bring my heart and spirit into a place of weakness and I am damaging my own future when I'm constantly focused on and worrying about the future.

On a recent day I spent several hours in the morning working. Close to noon I went to a bench on the water front. I sensed a leading to just observe. Five hours later, I was in the same spot and had experienced too many wonderful miracles to recount here. I was completely in the moment. Observing all of life around me, seeing, experiencing, hearing, feeling, touching, and smelling. The beauty was mesmerizing; the sounds became more and more beautiful as time went on. The feeling of wind blowing lightly on my skin, took on a life of its own. I was hearing conversations of people walking by with all of their stories and observing the ebb and flow of nature on glorious display for anyone to take notice.

Every moment an opportunity for God to speak, every second that passes so filled to the full with life. Those five hours were more filled with life then any five hours in recent memory. Angels came and went and truth and beauty poured into me continually. Miracles are happening all the time. We so often miss them because we aren't paying attention. They are happening now. Not in the past or future, but now.

We look at the past miracles and we idolize them, worship them, memorialize them, and we should. We look for miracles in our future; we pray for them, long for them, need them. But we can often miss them right in front of us right now. I mean literally right now.

As I am writing this and as you are reading it, miracles are happening, life is happening, God is speaking, beauty is unfolding; life is being created, renewed, and invigorated. Healing is taking place, spirits are moving, angels are ministering, abundant infinite miraculous life pouring into each and every moment all of the time.

As I sat there in this place of meditation and awareness, I became more and more connected to God and spirit as time passed. Do you ever wonder why, when you stop the flying wheel of your life and step off for a day or for an hour, and take time in silence, lay on the beach or walk in the park or close your eyes to escape for a while or any number of other ways to just be in the moment, that you always, without fail, feel better, relaxed, renewed, invigorated, more yourself, more in tune, in touch, connected, inspired. You tell yourself you need more of this, but life demands you back and you leave the moment and rush off into frenzy again.

When I was a minister for many years, I became intimately acquainted with the life of Jesus through the gospels. If we were to have an opportunity to recreate his life and to see him and watch him, we would see an unhurried, relaxed, in the moment, man, filled with a sense of purpose, and significance, and yet fully totally at all times experiencing the fullness of now.

Completely the opposite of accomplishing less because of such a life style, Jesus accomplished more in three years, then many many life times. He slowed down time and sucked up every moment of power and joy and love and grace, and truth and beauty and miracles and spirit and he never ever left the moment. This was the key to his power.

All spiritual leaders who have come into this world with a message from God were very similar in this respect. They were mystics who lived their lives on a different plan and one of the primary factors of what made them different is found in this idea of living fully present in the present moment. They all understood and communicated to us, that God was in the present, here and now and they compelled us to stop and look within and see in the silence, the reality of spiritual experience powerfully present like a rushing river within ever present and always abundant. Life transformation, healing, joy, and fullness, creative expression, life callings and purpose, faith and hope and eternity are found by the multitudes as they follow this powerful call to be still and know God and themselves truly in the present now.

When I'm living in the now, I become aware of a very powerful reality. My primary role in life is that of observer. As we shared earlier in our discussion about the power we have to choose which thoughts to attach to and which to reject, this is possible because we are in the moment as the observer watching our thoughts as they pass by.

The true me, the soul, is separate from my body and separate from my mind, I sit back this place of observation and see the world and experience the world through my senses. I'm doing nothing. In my true essence I'm being done, not doing. Sun shines upon my face, I feel the warmth, I am receiving it through my body, and my soul feels warm because my body feels warm.

My thoughts are this constant stream of consciousness flowing through my being just as real as the river and bay in front of me. I see them, I am separate from them, I allow some to pass and I pull some into me but it is a separate part of me then the mind, doing the act of observing and deciding which to allow and which to pass.

This is happening constantly. If we are living in awareness, we are simply aware of this reality and the power of it. When we do not live in the moment, we are not as in control of this process and we allow our minds to dictate what we will bring into us, we give up our soul's power to decide and when we do this we have far less power over our own lives.

While your life is unfolding in front of your eyes and as you are pursuing and projecting your dream, stay in the glorious moment. You will be more at peace, learn to trust God more, enjoy your life and the people in it more and ultimately you will find yourself moving much more fluently toward the unfolding that you are looking for.

NINETEEN

Love Is All There Is

"We are all born for love, it is the principle of existence and its only end."

Benjamin Disraeli

Everything in the life of the beautiful wanderer, all of it, if you want to narrow it down to one word, it is about love. Love is the essence of the power of the purpose of and the plan of God. We must know this if we are to find our way truly to the place that God intends. It is the highest peak of the spiritual journey, the place that everything else leads to and stems from, the place of love, for you, love for others and love for God.

There is a back bone and grounding to all of life and to all of the universal truth that we are learning and growing into, to all of the experiences that make up our beautiful wanderings. To all of our ups and downs, trials and errors, successes and joys, heart aches and pains, all of life is set on the foundation of one thing, the very universe and all that is in it and all the principles of it are based upon. That one thing is love.

Love is the power of all the energy force surging throughout the universe. It is what keeps the stars in their place, the earth in its orbit, the sun in its sustaining work. Love is the power that holds all things, sustains all things, infusing all things with life and purpose. If you take away love, you don't have evil or hate, you have nothing, nothing at all.

Evil and hate are simply forces that rise up to oppose love from time to time, but their very existence is in contrast to love and they only serve ultimately to demonstrate loves power and dominion overall. The possibility of evil in the universe had to exist in order for there to be love. Love is not love if it is the only condition available.

If I have no choice but to love then that stops being love immediately because love requires a choice to give myself to another, to be "in love." I must approach the object of potential love with a possibility of loving and a possibility of not loving, then I can follow my heart, my spirit, and love. I can then be absorbed with the beauty and truth and wonder of the object of my love and I can surrender my heart to giving affection to and doing well toward and demonstrating all the beauties that arise in the soul when we love. But I must have the option, the choice, or it will not be love. That option, or choice, creates the possibility of evil and we know well about its ugly history in the human experience.

However, we must keep it in proper perspective, we need to recognize its weakness in comparisons to loves power or else we will become overwhelmed by evil or hate and forget how much power we actually have to overcome.

Let me share an analogy. Love can be considered for this analogy like the law of gravity. It is an established, universal power, a principle build into the very fabric of things.

No one put it there, it is not the work of man or any other creature, we have nothing to do with its existence and yet we deal with its influence every moment of our life. It is a grounding force, keeping things in their order, giving foundation for life and for experience, allowing the platform for beauty and truth to be established upon its certainty. I can see the landscape because of gravity and I can experience the life giving power of earth and sun and sky because of gravity. I can experience you and you can experience me and we can live and move and have our being because of this power that holds all things and infuses all things with life.

We have in our desire to explore, discovered something called aerodynamics. This is a way for us to work against the power of gravity by creating a force that opposes it so that we can fly. Flying into the sky and sustaining flight in opposition to gravity. Gravity has allowed for and it will eventually serve to establish even more so, gravities supremacy. But for the moment of flight, it seems to be and is to some degree in opposition to gravity and succeeding in its rebellion!

This can occur for a period of time. Its occurrence may even give the impression that gravity is not supreme after all, that we may have been wrong about this and maybe there is another way to operate in the universe. Something happens though as time passes, fuel runs out to maintain the opposition and the force gives in to the power. Gravity brings the plane back down to earth and grounds it by its all-encompassing power. The power of gravity is just being itself; it is not fighting or pushing itself on the flying machines. It is just itself and it cannot be anything else. It is just operating as its creator enabled it to operate. It just so happens to be the power and the opposition to it, no matter how much it roars on its take off, will quietly come back down to earth eventually.

Love operates this way. Hate, evil may rise from time to time and it may appear that love has lost its grip, that maybe love isn't as supreme as we thought, that all of this talk about love being supreme and powerful maybe in question. Wisdom says wait and see. Watch what time will do, evil has to fight its way up and it has to maintain itself with anger and violence and rage and resentment.

All of these are destructive forces and will implode on themselves after time. The fuel will run out and love will once again reign when we can't go on and have nowhere else to turn.

Love will heal, forgive, renew, restructure, reconstitute, reconnect, reinvigorate, redirect, resurrect, and so so much more! Give love another chance. It will not let you down because it cannot fail, cannot stop loving, cannot be overcome, cannot be defeated, cannot be diminished, cannot be conditioned, cannot be decreased, and cannot be taken away.

Love is the universe and the universe is love, God is the source of the universe and God is love. Love is at the beginning and at the end and in every moment in between. Every star shines with love, every planet rotates for love, every life form lives in love, every energy molecule exists for love.

Each being must have love and give love in order to function properly. We were made by love and for love. When we operate outside of love we don't work well. We are sick and we are weak and we are not what we could be or should be. We know this intuitively when we are away from love. We know it on some soul level and we sense there is something very wrong. We are being drawn by loves power out of our darkness in this moment of realization.

Our ability to hide from love is very well documented. We have experienced pain because of evil or hate, we would rather be isolated them hurt again is our mentality. We don't want to love because a loving open heart is also open to hurt. This is so true; we will be hurt when we love because pain is a part of love. But the pain of isolating from love is far worse and it has no healing balm as an open heart does.

We must love, it is what we long for and what we are good at. It is not good for us to be alone. It doesn't mean we can't be alone and that we must be in an intimate relationship at all times, but it is not good for us to be disconnected from caring loving relationships where we can pour ourselves into others and others can pour themselves into us.

We know the fullness of life when we have the support and intimacy of love and we know the wretched loneliness when we do not. Why do our insides churn when we isolate? Why do we have to find mechanisms to escape from the pain of it? Because we need it and it needs us. I must have love, I must give love, and I must see and know that love is the very essence and purpose of my life, if I am to live in fullness in my journey.

The apostle said it most eloquently "If I speak in the tongues of men and angels but I do not have love, I am only a resounding gong or a clanging cymbal. If I have the gift of prophecy and can fathom all mysteries and all knowledge, and if I have a faith that can move mountains, but I do not have love, I am nothing, if I give myself to the poor and give over my body to hardship that I may boast, but do not have love, I gain nothing."

These words spell out what all of human history has confirmed and does to this very moment. Love is everything and if you have love you have everything and if you do not have love then you have nothing. This is what Jesus and Buddha and all enlightened souls through all ages have told us, this is the consistent and unifying message of all spiritual traditions of all ages.

If nations or religions or peoples groups or institutions or human endeavors of any kind are going to have any lasting impact and any ultimate value, it must be planted and intended and lived out in love.

This truth is the grounding of all of us! It brings us to the same level regardless of class or circumstance. We live in a world that distinguishes value based on such things as possessions or positions or popularity. When we do so we diminish the value structurally for those who do not fit the mold that we have set. When we have people in our cities living on the streets and when we have children who do not have food to eat, something is very very wrong and we know it.

We have left our grounding and we are heading for a crash. When we understand love and the principles of love and how they are the ground of all, we will not allow this to be the case. The extent of human suffering, unrelieved is a clear barometer to how grounded or ungrounded we are in love.

Have you looked in the mirror and stared long enough to notice there is really a real person looking back at you? Have you ever had that strange and a little weird experience? It can be a little disconcerting when you realize that you have just stared a hole right through yourself! Sometimes when this happens, you quickly look away. You don't want to be exposed to yourself. You might look back timidly to catch a glimpse. What is this discomfort all about?

We feel a little judged, exposed, not comfortable, yet curious enough to look back. When I look back, I notice me, fully attentive and waiting for the return stare to be reconnected. It is an awkward exchange. Most of the time we escape this awkwardness, we quickly dart away from the mirror and go about our day.

What happened in that moment? What made us feel so uncomfortable and yet drawn to go back? What if we had stayed in the ethereal experience and not broken eye contact with ourselves when we began to feel our own soul looking back? It has something to do with our self-awareness, our self-love.

Most of us don't know ourselves very well. We have images of ourselves that we project to others which take years to construct. We have images of ourselves projected to us from others. Sometimes we have competing self-images. What we wish we were, and what we think we are. Without spending time in self-awareness which is really nothing more than getting to know ourselves, we are never really sure.

If someone asked you what makes you happy, what you love, what do you want in life; you might not be able to answer clearly. You have gotten so used to the mixed up images of yourself that you don't really have clarity about such questions so you would rather not address them. We stay busy, dull the soul's appeals and go about our life business. Sometimes pain and hurt buries the possibility of self-awareness even further into the soul.

If I have been hurt, then any conversation with me about myself just brings up all the hurt that I have or am burying. My self-blame or anger and resentment toward someone else, or my guilt or shame, and many other negative emotions have to have a release or resolution without a look in the mirror to learn about you.

This is why therapy can be such a healing experience. We are in essence, enabled to look in the mirror and not pull the stare away, at least for the hour that we have committed to this focus. So much hurt and mistreatment stems from my not knowing the person within, burying my hurt and being uncomfortable with the person in the mirror. I act out my own self-image on other people. If I don't like myself very much, eventually I find ways to convince myself that you don't like me. If I feel hurt, I will hurt others, if I am afraid of confronting myself, I will isolate from others and resist deep connections.

Everything in my life is affected by my self-image. A large part of my experience in growing as a person on this beautiful journey is growing back in love with me. I emanate from a being of pure love and am loved completely and unlimited by God, I have had to learn how to not love myself and therefore I have to relearn how to. The truth is, God expects nothing from me and loves me without any conditions or expectations, period. But I set up a system because of my lack of self-love, where God could be let down or pleased by my actions or lack thereof.

God does not judge us and calls us to not judge one another, but when we don't allow love to penetrate our inner selves, we judge ourselves all the time as unworthy and therefore we assume God is that way and we become that way toward others. When we love ourselves we are taking God and others off the hook so to speak. We are letting it be known that we are taking control of and responsibility for our own lives.

When we do this we actually find God's love flooding in the now open heart that had been closed to it before. We see that we are lovable because we have discovered this in loving ourselves. We also find others, those who really love us for who we are and not for what we have done or can do for them, loving us and staying in our lives.

We find angels and messengers of love all over the place when we open our hearts to self-love. We find nature singing songs to us and we see the stars shinning their light for us. We hear the rain as it gently soaks into the earth and we realize its falling for us, we understand that the sun sets in beautiful radiance for us and the new day dawns so that we can awaken to new opportunities to be loved.

Our inner world changes dramatically, the anxiety and pressure of performance slowly ebbs away like fog burning off as the sun rises. We slowly begin to see the light and feel the warmth within, this is what love feels like. Like a warm fire on a cold day or a soothing drink when parched by heat. Our soul begins to rise up to the nutrient of love being poured on her dry soils. When we begin to love ourselves, something very spiritual happens and our journey takes on a beauty that no wandering tale can compare to. A door has opened to God that will flow with such a powerful force and abundance that everything in you and about you will be changed.

It may take some time to unlearn certain patterns in your life and to set new parameters and expectations for yourself and others. It may take some serious changes in your life to adjust the outside to the new inner reality, but all that needs to change will change because love has a power all its own that cannot be defeated or resisted once the flood gates have been opened. One powerful reality that will feel almost overwhelming is the idea that it doesn't depend on you! You do not have to fix yourself or anyone else; you do not have to hang on for dear life anymore, to self-imposed and unrealistic expectations.

To allow self-love into your life, it is not a doing that is called for, it is a being. Being your true self, letting go of all the expectations, and let downs because of those expectations and hurts and blaming and judgements. All of it let it go. It's ok, that you aren't perfect and that you fail and that you don't always feel like it and that you doubt and are afraid. Did you hear that? It's ok. Love doesn't care about all of that, it only cares about you. Not what you do or have done, or will or could do.

Love loves you, as you are, pure essence of you, beautiful wanderer, Unique and wonderful you. You are loved just like this now, completely and forever. Look back into that mirror, this time smile back at yourself! Accept all of it, all of you. Tell yourself, you deserve love, you are loved, and you are love. Let it in, let it fill you and flow into all parts of you.

Forgive yourself, be tender to yourself, take care of yourself, do something you enjoy, for yourself. Start putting you first, start taking care of yourself first, get the right amount of rest, eat properly, exercise, meditate, pray, write, read, enjoy, experience, live. It's your life, no one else's. Let others live their lives, you live yours. If we don't love we are not representing God because God is love. We know this because we see that the foundational need of all creation is love and if all creation emanates from its source which we are calling God then this source must logically be love is its very essence.

Beauty comes from love, truth comes from love, life comes from love, goodness comes from love, giving comes from love, creative expressions come from love. God is love and we are sparks of God made in the likeness of divine nature. We require love therefore because we are love. This is why when we begin to open ourselves to love; we are opening ourselves to our very nature, our origins, and our source of being.

It is profound and life changing because it is so significant. The difference that self-love will make in your life and mine is the difference between living in fullness or emptiness, living with joy or sadness, living in abundance or want, it is night and day, life or death and any other extreme analogy you can add to this. God can be found inside of you when you love yourself. You begin to rise to your own significance and potential not for love but from love. See the difference? It's a universe of difference. It is everything.

We can love others as much or as little as we choose and it has very little to do with their response to us or lack of it. Because we have experienced love for ourselves we find it a natural flow to love others. Inner love cannot stay inside for long, it must be expressed. The world is desperate for love and if you and I are filled with love we become an instrument of love to the world, multitudes of opportunities will come to the beautiful wanderer to offer love to others. The world will change if enough of us fall in love and offer love to the world.

One of the primary reasons for my existence is to love others. When in love with myself and having the love of God flowing through me, I am filled to a new fullness by pouring love into you. No one needs love more than when they deserve it the least.

Nothing can lift a person out of their brokenness and despair like love; nothing can heal the ills of humanity like love. A movement of love is what we need. Let's be a part of such a movement.

TWENTY

I Am Possible

What is impossible with man is possible with God.

As I conclude my thoughts on this life of spiritual realities and how you and I traverse it in our wanderings, I do so with the most important truth along the way. We simply can never say that anything in life is impossible because of the reality that the great I AM presence of God is with us at all times in all places and will never cease to be.

If there is anything that should be completely obvious to us as we have journeyed through these pages, it should be this all-encompassing truth. Faith is the substance of things hoped for, the evidence of things not seen. God has a methodology of calling those things which are not as though they are! Clearly God is a God of the impossible! This is the normal operating procedure of the spiritual realm, thus, experiences, like omens, and synchronicities and miracles, divine interventions, occur in our lives as we walk along the wandering path toward our spiritual fulfilment. Yes, the truth is that our lives present many many challenges.

We have spent some time articulating them. We all have those seasons of deep suffering and trials and often feel the hopelessness that comes with those seasons. However, they are not sent for any other reason than to allow us to experience the realization once again, that I Am Possible! That I can overcome, even this!! That I am stronger than I realized, because of God's presence in my life. That I am a child of God and the very creation of this powerful, glorious divine being that is the epicenter of all life and consciousness!

I am filled with dreams and yes, often those dreams are beyond my background or credentials or expectations that others have placed upon me or my own expectations for myself. God has greater dreams for you then you could even imagine. The divine word is that God is able to do exceedingly abundantly above all that we could ask or think according to the power that works in us!; I know the plans I have for you says the lord, plans to prosper you and to bless you and to give you hope! In ancient times, one of Gods servants, no different than you or me, once prayed "Lord would you bless me indeed, and enlarge my territory and let your hand be with me and keep me from all evil!! And the Lord granted him that which he requested!"

Remember, it is Gods dream, placed in you, it becomes yours by this transference, and you pray it back to God, express it in your longings and desires, share it in your creativity and gifts, and it becomes your life! But it started in the dream of God for you! Would you be so bold as to make this prayer of the obscure Jabez, your own? Would you believe the truth that I Am Possible?! That your greatest dreams for yourself have not even touched the surface of God's dreams for you?

The things that cause us to doubt this truth, that cause us to stumble before it and turn back, are always related to my feelings of unworthiness or inadequacy, what others may think or say or my own experiences of failures. Yet none of these criteria matches the word of God and the promise that divine mandate has determined. Would you choose to believe yourself, others, circumstances, or God? I see with limited scope and my sight is affected by so many factors that I have limited control over, the opinions of others has even less to do with the reality of potential in my life, and circumstances are nothing but the result of the previous season of expectations and intentions that I have projected into the spiritual universe. My failures certainly bear little resemblance to the true nature of me.

They are simply markers of what not to do in the future or memorials to seasons where I learned to trust more and fear less. God's assessment of me is infallible and unlimited in scope. Omniscience is at the disposal of the divine mind so there isn't anything left to chance or information that might set the train off the tracks around the corner. Do you see that God, who says you can do all things, knows that there is truly nothing impossible for you because of divine involvement in your life?

I AM is the name God gives to divine nature for us to understand that God is always present in the moment, in us and in full measure of divinity. If I AM is with you and sending you as was the case with Moses and is the case with each and every one of us. Then, we are never alone, never on our own, never without help, support, love, power, forgiveness, new mercies, grace, faith, strength, wisdom, healing, provision, abundance, and anything else you could possibly need! Whatever it is that you need in your life at this moment, whatever it is add it to my list and even make your own.

Whatever you require or need, God is! And God is with you and is in you and is you! You are the spark of God the candle of the lord, the very temple of God.

God looks out of your eyes, touches with your hands, hears with your ears and speaks with your tongue. God is in the midst of you and God is all around you at all times!

The spiritual journey that I am calling in this work Beautiful Wanderer, is a journey of yes and amen, a journey of dreams accomplished and hearts desires realized, it is a happy ending every time because it always ends with God, period! So, there is absolutely nothing to fear, accept to live life not knowing that this is true and allowing yourself to be blinded into thinking that you are so much less then you really are. If there is nothing else that I accomplish in the writing of this book and the sending it out into the world, I want to accomplish this, that you might, after reading, know, at a very deep level, that you are much much more then you thought you were, and that you might get to work like never before, partnered with God and supported by an entire universe that will assist you, in realizing your life's callings and dreams and living out the fullness of who you are, you are a beautiful wanderer and that beauty, needs to be shared with the world. You need to be shared with the world! The world is so much more beautiful when you bloom and blossom and so much brighter when you shine forth your light!

There will be a day soon coming when you will see the light shining and the vibrant colors of you and wonder, is that really coming from me!! Oh what a day that will be! I can't wait for it! That is the day that this book is written for and my prayer is that this work will promote that kind of experience in lives many times over! I am experiencing the accomplishment of my own dream when that happens for you, and ultimately it is Gods dream for both of us being fulfilled and there is divine celebration that is above and beyond our own.

When you finish this book, step outside, look up into the sky, see God in everything, see yourself in God and see yourself as the spark of God! Live it!! Live it to the full! Let nothing or no one stop you! Graciously but boldly be single minded and set your face with determined focus on the prize of the high calling that you have! I can't wait to see what happens next!!

With Love,

Tony Gilotte

Recommendations

"I feel like I am experiencing a cup of warm Earl Gray tea for the first time, sipping your words and admiring the depth of character, closing my eyes to absorb the meaning and cherish the flavor. "

Kate Besse.
Author and Life Coach

"I have been blessed to read chapters of this gorgeous book 'Beautiful Wanderer' by Tony Gilotte and each time I immerse myself in Tony's World I feel uplifted, restored and spiritually held. Tony's gift of communing with our Beloved Creator and translating Divine Wisdom for us to read is an absolute blessing to the World! I highly recommend its' reading and use as a powerful spiritual guide in today's World... "

Andrea Lee Fisher
Singer/ Song Writer/
Spiritual Coach

Made in the USA
Middletown, DE
26 April 2016